CLAIR-OBSCUR OF THE SOUL

BY

JEAN-YVES SOLINGA

FIRST EDITION

Little Red Tree Publishing, LLC,
635 Ocean Avenue, New London, CT 06320

DEDICATIONS

I dedicate this book to my wife Elaine for her love, friendship and steadfast presence.

Also to my children Robert and Nicole who represent in my heart the best in my faith in the future.

To my sister Marie Louise and brother Pierre who have been not only loving siblings but have also offered me the caring privilege and comfort of a second set of parents.

To the memory of my father Marcel and my mother Anna who taught me to love life through their own example.

Copyright © 2008 Jean-Yves Solinga

Manufactured in USA

First Edition 2008

Cover and Book Design:
Michael John Linnard, MCSD

Front Cover paintings and photograph:

1. Extract from *Girl with a Pearl Earring* (1665-1675) by Johannes Vermeer (Public domain).
2. Extract from *Marat Assassinated* (1793) by Jacques-Louis David (Public domain).
2. Two extracts from *The Night Watch* (1642) by Rembrandt Harmenszoon van Rijn (Public domain).
4. Photograph of the Eiffel Tower (free download from Eiffel Tower Official web site) by Philippe Bourgeois.

Back Cover paintings:

1. Extract from *The Night Watch* (1642) by Rembrandt Harmenszoon van Rijn (Public domain).
2. Extract from *Portrait of Jan Six* (1654) by Rembrandt Harmenszoon van Rijn (Public domain).
3. Extract from *Girl With a Pearl Earring* (1665-1675) by Jahannes Vermeer (Public domain).
4. Extract from *The Milkmaid* (1658-1660) by Johannes Vermeer (Public domain)..
5. Extract from *The Fighting Téméraire Tugged to her Last Berth to be Broken* (1839) by J M W Turner (Public domain).

Library of Congress Cataloging-in-Publication Data:

Solinga, Jean-Yves
   Clair-Obscur of the Soul / by Jean-Yves Solinga. -- 1st ed.
      p. cm.
   Includes glossary.
   Includes index.
   ISBN-13: 978-0-9789446-3-6 (pbk. : alk. paper)
   I. Title.
   PS3619.O4326C55 2008
   811'.6--dc22
                                    2008016334

Little Red Tree Publishing, LLC
635 Ocean Avenue,
New London, CT 06320
website: www.littleredtree.com

CONTENTS

Chapter 4 – Daydream

Chapter 5 – Voices

Chapter 6 – Between the Friend and the Lover

Chapter 7 – Dreams and Realities

FOREWORD

It is without doubt a privilege for Little Red Tree Publishing, LLC, of New London, to publish this collection of poems called *Clair-obscur of the Soul* by Jean-Yves Solinga.

Following the success of an earlier publication of poetry by Jon Norman called *Days of Creativity,* edited by James Stidfole, we were inundated with submissions for publication from many aspiring writers and poets. Amongst these submissions was one from Jean-Yves that stood out because of its intensity, lyricism and insight into the essence of what it is to be human, in fact beyond and through to the heart and soul.

As I read Jean-Yves's poems I immediately became aware that here before me was a previously unpublished poet with an effortless ability to use language, conveying myriad emotions, an ambience of mellifluous subtlety with immense depth from the very first poem. As I read further poems the accumulated effect built into a powerful poetic statement. Jean-Yves's free prose style of poetry, which eschews more traditional forms, is not in the least affected or pretentious but rather it is immanent to his expansive vision and narrative voice as a poet.

The title and many of the poems in this book draw you into a world of intellectual contrasts and duality, where one reality is juxtaposed with another, that are simultaneously fascinating, unsettling and revelatory. This is unsurprisingly reflected in the poet's life story, which is filled with an inherent cultural duality: part colonial French-Morocco and part American-Anglo Saxon. Jean-Yves metaphorically refers to this as "solar" and "Labrador" or the sun of North Africa and the cold ocean current off the New England coast line.

Jean-Yves Solinga was born in Algeria of French parents and moved to Morocco as a young boy where he spent an idyllic childhood and at 14 was abruptly removed and brought to America by his family. He was subsequently called up and served in the US Army and was honorably discharged, then became a teacher. He spent his entire career teaching French Culture and Literature in Connecticut schools and colleges. After the death of his father he married and raised a family, completing a Masters and PhD before retiring in 2004 and then simply began earnestly to write poetry.

Therefore, I present this stunning book and debut from a poet who has lived a life of cultural duality and through some of the major social upheavals of the 20th century, writing from the depths of his soul. A remarkable book of poetry that must be read by all those interested in a singularly unique view of life that may re-define the capacity of poetry to be what it should be: the art of expressing pure thought about the existential human condition.

Michael Linnard, CEO
New London, CT 2008

INTRODUCTION

I suppose, like many aspiring poets, I have at times written on anything that was at hand and put those thoughts away in piles on shelves. We write for the love of it not expecting to be necessarily read outside of a small circle. Therefore, being published for the first time is both an honor and an unsettling experience.

I think it appropriate here to begin by offering a brief explanation or rationale if you will for the poems in this book and by default the poet I am. I have written poetry in one form or another for many years while busying myself with the trials and tribulations of a career in education and academia to earn a living and provide for myself and a family. The sum total of my best efforts I lay before you in this book and hope that it meets your expectation of what a poet should achieve.

My cultural identity, which is inextricably bound to my poetry, has two faces: one French and the other Anglo-Saxon. I think, speak, and write fluently in both languages and consequently bring the lyricism of one to the direct and acoustical strength of the other.

Also as a result of my love of the process of ideas through philosophy and literature that seek to develop and express the human consciousness in its own humanity, much of the substance of this collection of poems lives in that other place in our lives: on the borders of reality. It is the pliable setting of fiction: the unreal, the surreal, and the fantasy of imagination.

It is a place that can turn a beach into a tactile state of mind; a city into an architectural statement about worldly appetites; a simple cup of coffee into a Proustian key to a fable about the heart; an emergency room near-death experience into a quasi Classic Greek stage with real as well as romanticized images.

It is the product of a mixture, a 'pastiche' of pieces of things and people around the writer. Who is sitting next to him, and what it could mean. It can also be somewhere else: a dream, an obsession. The daily ingredients of a teaching profession do not make for excitement. The intricacies of the past participle agreement in the passé composé do not inspire poetry.

And so, one jumps to the other side: away from things that are proper, bourgeois, and repetitive. Of course you make use of some of the material at hand. You write about what you know or think you know. Flaubert is reputed to have found the general structure of *Madame Bovary* in a newspaper article; so much of his life was of little interest! But he used observations of his father's medical profession for one of the best written passage of western literature. The artist acts often like the descendants of these cultures that have managed to use whatever was at hand, no matter how meager or eclectic, to build a pathos in their lives and preciously meaningful jewelry.

There is, generally speaking, a conducting wire, a conscious leitmotif, in my poetry. It is built with an overarching design. It follows a slightly flawed man of letters and deconstructs him in front of us. He is susceptible to the temptations of sight. His glance and the glance of others upon him are both fertile opportunities and abysses of dangers. We follow him back to Paris and relive with him the introduction, reintroduction, magic, happiness and despair in this city. With mostly no absolute external or traditional moral guidance, he tries to live in a world of good conscience, a world of rules where the divinities have appropriated libertine exceptions for themselves and leave us panting, as voyeurs, for the same chance.

With him, we dream of his Magreban past and his idealistic return to this warm site of childhood. With him, we experience the splintered existence of being uprooted from culture to culture, from landscape to landscape. He sees multiple reflections of Others in the mirror.

On the margins of society is where the interesting tensions exist. The infractions of the rules and presence of taboos are like the voltage that make us want to jump the gap, between what is proper and normal, to the other side where the gratuitous, this figure of happiness, resides.

A car driving through a dark landscape in New England is a long way from the Medieval world of Tristan and Isolt; but the mind and the heart are well suited for the trip. The late teenage rebellion of Romeo and Juliet would only be a chronicle of Italian Renaissance without the couple's disregard for parental fiat and its tragic result. The great Jean Baptiste Racine of French Classic Tragedies, in *Phèdre*, would have had to invent uncontrolled and uncontrollable lust in order to make us understand the self-destructive Queen's love for her step child.

So we are at the inception of these strange discoveries and rediscoveries in the souls of the beings in these pages. It is the very consciousness of good and evil that makes them and us struggle: and this is good for art. The authenticity of their pain and anguish is not reduced because it takes place in the world of artistic fiction. If art is the vehicle to give a moment, a sigh, a glance, a degree of immortality, so much the better.

All moments, real, inspired from reality or otherwise taken from family sources, are doomed to become part of the past. But if the fiction of art offers a temporal extension to these moments, on a museum canvas, a melody, in lines of poetry, then let us enjoy vicariously the intersection and overlapping of the solidity of life on the plasticity of fiction.

Between North Africa and New England exists the landscape of many of these poems. In Arabic, Sidi Moussa is the Moses of the Bible: the patron saint of the wanderer.

The coldness of the Labrador current haunts these lines along with images of Sidi Moussa in the warm setting that surrounded the youth of the narration. It is, more specifically, the name of a miniscule beach north of Salé in Morocco.

Bi-polar would therefore be an appropriate descriptive for this poetic world. It is a world torn between languages and cultures. It craves for absolutes with the conviction of an atheist. And with a Faustian fever, it thirsts for youth with impending decrepitude on the horizon.

The themes sneak their way through two worlds: one, of the thematic universality of Classicism, and the other, that of the very personal individualistic emphasis of Romanticism.

It is when these worlds are in complementary equilibrium - one person versus society, the first person singular versus plural, the lonely artist at his desk versus his audience in a full theatre - that the words, the painting, the artistic expression break out of the solidity of the present and make the future reader or viewer still hold his breath.

The best art is the one that has the feel of authenticity. Of personal immediacy of the writer, as well as the capacity to allow the viewer to take possession of a piece of it.

The way that one walks with glazed eyes through museums and looks nonchalantly at a painting; returns and then stops breathlessly as though he had painted the scene himself in another life. Or the unease caused by a scenario of a movie that seems to put a piece of our life on the screen: that line where classicism, in its eternal applications, meets romanticism, in its intimate and personal projection on the viewer.

Even when the expression is circumstantial and personal, it is especially in the way the reader eventually sees herself or himself in the text that can give relevance and ultimately value to the poem. One, for instance, does not have to know personally the dissolute life of the Paris of Baudelaire to understand the void of his soul.

And so it is that, like Baudelaire or Camus, I use religious artifacts and references to build antithetical contrasts with the fleshy amoral present.

The plasticity of an *understandable* language is what guided me: both in French and English. Because of this view of language in general and my cultural background in particular, I have used a nontraditional poetic versification and poetic meter. I have a particular affection for free verse and lyrical prose style.

In defense of my choice of poetic form and lyrical structure I quote from the last speech of Trepliov in Checkov's play *The Sea Gull*: "I'm coming more and more to the conclusion that it's a matter not of old forms and not of new forms, but that a man writes, not thinking at all of what form to choose, writes because it comes pouring out from his soul."

Some poems came to me only in English and many have remained as such: sometimes because of the circumstance of their genesis or the depth of their cultural links.

In an absurd world, I find mankind's inflated view of itself to be the beautiful driving force behind much of what we would understand as art. And that is all right. And that is good.

For art, in all its forms, is the most generous act of solidarity. And even when hurtful eternal and personal truths must be described, art and the artist can and must find ways to make it beautiful in its expression.

Yes, I still believe in art for art sake.

In the final analysis, poetic beauty is the by-product of the drive on the part of the artist to stabilize the ephemeral. It is in the pursuit of that certain glance on that particular afternoon - that makes the artist want to stop time in time.

And, as is often said of the surprising regeneration found in Picasso's art, it is, in my view, the ultimate joy of success to be able to recreate it through the "eyes of a child" as though it were seen or felt for the first time.

Finally I would like to acknowledge and express my deepest appreciation to Michael Linnard of Little Red Tree Publishing. Michael has proven to have an uncanny sensitivity and understanding of my poetry to which he also brought an enormous dedication to making this beautiful publication possible.

In sharing this poetry with the outside world for the first time, Michael has also allowed me to hope that the experience of the reader will be as meaningful and heartfelt as it was in the writing of it.

Jean--Yves Solinga
Gales Ferry, CT 2008

Jean-Yves Solinga 2008

(above) A photograph taken in Salé, Morocco, in 1948. From left to right: my sister, Marie Louise, whom I called "maman Malou" since I considered her my other mother. My mother whom I called "maman-maman." And my brother Pierre who would use his first money prize to buy me a toy. I was privileged, in that way, to always feel loved. My hair would be cut to boy's length within a year I hasten to add.
(Jean-Yves Solinga collection)

CHAPTER 1

BACK TO SID MOUSSA

These poems are essentially reflections of the Morocco of my youth and its relationship with the present.

Some of these poems take a circuitous 'bio-fictional' road through the cold waters of the "Labrador" current: "In America... dreaming of Morocco" and "On the Gray Sands of the Labrador." The former poem refers to a bas-relief scene of Sahara Bedouins sleeping under their tents. This picture was in the living room of our friends in Salé and ironically was but just a few miles from the real thing at that time. I have remembered, on this wall, the distillation of reality through the years. The latter imagines names written in the cold sands of New England being carried back to the Atlantic coast of North Africa.

You also find a sunny Provence in "On the Way to Saint Pierre" and "Avenue des roches," with its cicadas, fish market, Corniche and Château d'If of Monte Cristo fame.

North Africa is an integral part of "Silence of the Souls" and "Between the Handsome Spahi and the Leather Satchel." It is a setting in front of which my father and his friend try to forget about the war years, drinking their aromatic Pastis under the sun of Morocco. In the latter, the remaining symbols of one's life contradict and speak for the dying image on a hospital bed.

Physical pieces of the past are at the root of some of the reconstruction of these years. Such things as a lithograph of the church on the hill top of Marseille. The leather pouch of my father. A snapshot of the unsightly "reality" of a contemporary view of Sidi Moussa, north of the capital of Rabat: "The Death of Sidi Moussa" and "The Storks in Morocco" are emblematic of my daily winter sight. A picture as a new immigrant on the streets of New York shows me as a young man seemingly ready for the challenges: "Avenue des roches."

The adage that one cannot go back home is symbolically 'served' in "Between the Mother Hen and her Son" in which my pet rooster ends up in a couscous as my family prepares to leave the land that I had appropriated with the love that only daily familiarity, akin to Karen Dinesen's *Out of Africa*, brings into the soul of a youngster and remains forever.

It is inevitable that a stream of melancholia runs through this chapter; but it is, hopefully, the source of authentic sentiments through verbal imagery that can be universally appreciated.

CHIAROSCURO OF THE SOUL

On the wall of a kitchen...
 ...in the middle of the maroon-warm color of the cabinets...
  ...while a black rain fills the windy emptiness full of autumn...

On the wall of a kitchen...
 ...surrounded by a frame of black and silver...
  ...lives quietly an image that joins the past to the future.

In front of this image...
 ...the canvas of my uprooted soul defines itself in streaks of clair-obscur.

The maternal cultural cloth is left with only rips and alterations...
 ...and it would be easier to just fold it upon a self of the past...
  ...to forget it and rejoin the things of the living present.

But the perverted after-taste of nostalgic contradictions and contrasts keep its sweet-sour taste on my lips.
Between things... I have been placed... and not in the middle... between them shall I remain.

In the beginning... there was the deadly cold of the streets, which had replaced the generous Provencal and Maghreban universe.
An omnipresent cold, contradicted by the traditions brought along in our luggage still touched by the Mediterranean pines.

Meals eaten under the purple insignia of wine... while the multitudes on the other side of the door cleaned themselves in milk and puritan baths.

The linguistic ambiguity that always brings you back to the anguish filled first vision of Liberty in an early morning fog of New York harbor...
...and the feeling that one had left on board something precious and personal before descending to the dock.

This emotional chiaroscuro is made up of, too often languorous and too long-lasting, idealized glances of the Maghreban mirage.
Warm and red remembrances of the enormous walls of the Kasbah of Salé.
Of its fried food smells... and especially... especially... the corruption of the senses and the precious smell of the bread cooked in the neighborhood ovens.

While on the other side of the Atlantic... were waiting for us the first joys of the first crystalline and virginal sensations of the first snow of the New World.

Between the red walls of the Kasbah and the powdery frigidity... we will have well transplanted the body... but not the soul...

2

...for... one...

...will have learned to live off the nourishment from this new earth...

...while the other will have only sighs that will get stronger with age.

And since... all these pebbles were rolling in my shoes.
Sending these stones from left to right under the bottom of the foot...

...I was walking as best I could...

...I had resigned myself...

...I had lost long ago my right of return... among those things that would recognize me.

Until the moment when... in front of this image... made of ochre colors and naïve simplicity...
...all of that dissolved with this representation in front of which I had so often walked during the day.

Just some reproduction... of a long ago forgotten ceremony.
An old and ridiculous style... which by its incongruous presence on this wall in the Americas... brings me back... and will bring me back... to the only place that will give me peace.

An enormous irony prevails everywhere...

...in this mundane and practical place..

...in front of a stainless sink full of dirty dishes...

...in this atheistic heart... face to face with this pious image...

I had stopped... astonished... my eyes captured by the maritime pine on the right, on a hill of l'Estaque... and on the left the silhouette of the *Good Mother*.

And while I was looking without religious conviction upon this image of Notre Dame de la Garde...

...I felt for the first time since almost always...

...something in me that knew where... and why...

...I will find again the hole left behind by my wanderings.

IN AMERICA… DREAMING OF MOROCCO

Outside is snow
And I think of sand

Outside is cold
I think of a painting

It hangs in my youth

Warmth is its subject
Warm is its memory

Sahara was its setting

Gone are its owners

So is the sand.

VOLUBILIS

Magically, with only silence around him,
Except for the cracking of the brittle snow
And the play of Moonlight on the vibrating ice crystals,

The scaly reflections transformed themselves into those of sand,
In the oppressive heat around the Roman city of Volubilis .

He remembered, in his youth, his surprise
Facing the inorganic dryness of the landscape,
Seemingly fighting human intrusion:

"Why build a city here?" He had asked his father.

Heat and void had the whole flatness to themselves.
Man-made objects had a temporary and unstable wavy value.

It was as though the black ribbon of the road
Could at any time be swallowed
In the heat of disappearing mirages.

Not too far away, a glimpse of the cold green
Of the Atlantic Ocean in the ochre of this bled of bleds.
His glance and senses trying to reconstruct, among these ruins,
The living, the dead and the emptiness.

A lesson was corporally and tactilely imposed on him,
Walking up the steps from the Forum,
Towards the remnants of a Temple.

The rounded curves in the center of each step
Marked the 'Memory' encased in the stone.

The innumerable leather soles had rounded them
With the imprints of feet, long ago vanished.

How to reconcile this petrified city, previously inhabited?
What of the humanity within it?

How could there now be only the noise of the sun
And the rustling of vipers?
What was the role of these abandoned columns?
What part was of man? What part was of nature?

All the weight of things seemingly assembled
In this majestically... 'inhumane'... 'nonhuman,' place.

Voices of tourists seemed to die over the ruins.
A blanket above them allowed nature to be left alone.

They were pitiful figures in front of these solid shafts
Of the world of stone.

Man had tried by the erection of these proud columns
To architecturally stop Time in Time.

These same columns previously covered with marble,
Now naked in front of them.

Under the rapid and chaste glance of tourists,
They were revealing too much of their weaknesses.

The hard staircase steps had allowed themselves
To be impregnated by pieces of the past:
Being made smooth under the softness of the leather of sandals.

Somewhere in all that solidity remained the hope
Of molecular presence persisting in Space and Time.

THE DEATH OF SIDI MOUSSA

The advantage of the gods is their immortality:
Decreed in a moment of weakness by mankind.

Your landscape, Sidi Moussa, more fragile,
Is inhabited by my remembrance linked only
To the shiver of my molecules.

Through your very name and your Temple
I chose to see a solidity of an absolute left behind.

You were the intermediary between the thirst of the soul
That would bring me, one day, to see you again,
And the sweet waters that satisfy the body
After a messianic travel and the fervor of dreams.

Between the endless walk
And the rest under the date tree,
Is inevitable death.

But there are deaths
That leave us only with red eyes
And a lost glance on what we have lost

On the other hand, there are deaths
That stop everything living in life.

That leave us only with what is front of us
And nothing behind.

Having heard of your death,
Among the greasy wrappers and the rats,
Among the various forms of plastic,
Among the dirt and Time,

Things that I did not know how to stop

I decree, You, in turn,
And thanks to your little white beach,

Inapproachable, precious and forever perfect.

Upon news of author's idealized little beach of Youth a generation later.

THE STORKS IN MOROCCO

Burns: of Summer ocher and soil.
Heat: of brown dry mud.
Soil: cracked, running with black pointed ants,
Scorpions, and vipers.

And then, rains of Autumn
Softening things
Like an oil of youth.

Shivers on the top of newly freed, crazed grass.
Renewal of the Maghreban humidity.

Return of sounds of the northern birds
And the fresh winds of the coast.

But nothing official until the return
On the roof of the house across
Of the storks from Alsace.

My adult snow encased glance
Reconstructs now my presence in this landscape
Made of crystals of heat.
With a little boy in the middle of things.

A black and white feathered couple
Silhouetted against a back drop of remembrance
And a chimney corner.

Precarious promontory and clacking of beaks
Announcing a joy in the nest

The years would follow each other
With my impression that these animals would,
By their very presence, make the seasons turn.

Leaving me envious now of their descendants
Who contrary to me, remain today close to this site
Where I first saw their parents

ON THE WAY TO SAINT-PIERRE

Silently separated from the other neighborhoods,
Far from the venerable shouts of the fish market of the Vieux Port,

Toward the pine-scented essence of Saint-Loup,
These walls always appeared to me as proudly different from all others.

More than autonomous... as though they did not need to go to Others.
They knew that Others would come to them.

They waited patiently in a rocky mutism:
Of gray slabs and rusty doors,
Of aligned chestnut trees and forgotten flowers.

Upon its approach... view of whitish hills,
Denying, by their color of snow, the heat of summer visits.

And the eternal cicadas... outside of mortal time...
...the one and true presence not to disappear from this setting.

We go back there after solemn nuptials and circumstantial ties.
The broken hearts of some and the unfaithfulness of others.

The uncontrolled laughter of champagnes of first communion and promotion.
Of wise decisions and passing happiness.

Of travel separations and various lifestyles.
Of reconciliations, after family whispers, behind jealous doorways.

Of a Paris full of Verlaine still under its Romantic rain.
Of Anglo snows from the Labrador leading to cravings of the mother tongue
and of images of Pagnol.

And with the years we find ourselves returning there on pilgrimages.
To this spot of respectful tranquility and of Mistral-swept diamond-clear
eternal skies,
We walk up alleys that recognize in our silence,
The silence of years of silence.

As though our steps found again the lost steps of lost years.
We lose ourselves in it... gently...
We feel comfortable, enveloped in protection in spite of our internal atheism.

We recognize a name among the letters losing their relief,
A fountain, a statue whitened by the suns.

A reciprocal peace reigns.
And while we follow once more this ritual,
We cannot avoid the bittersweet self-awareness,

Of seeing ourselves accompanied... by our friends and close ones...
...one last time on this same path.

In the meantime, all that is left for us, is to live in the knowledge...
that we will all return,
The day of our day... on the Way to Saint-Pierre.

"Here I am, once more, on the Way to visit Saint-Pierre." Upon news from family in France announcing their presence in this cemetery for a funeral service.

ON THE GRAY SANDS OF THE LABRADOR

On the gray sands... under the timid Labrador sun... live two names.
Like two reddish wounds on a surface rendered ever virginal by the wind...
...they write in sinuous forms...
        ...the drawing of a passion without tomorrow.

With minuscule mounds and valleys... they think themselves safe from the tides.
They verbalize... in arabesques representing the form of fertile hips and curves...
...the eternal sensuality face to face with a drab puritan sky.

Scratched in the grating thousand year old silicon with a dead reed twig...
...the loving letters marry and intertwine with each other without shame in
spite of the cool wind.

On the gray sands of the Labrador exist two names...
...they are but a few steps from the waves...
        ...which teach us... by their presence...
        ...the wise lesson that consciousness learns face to face with the temporal.

On the smooth sands of the Labrador used to exist two names...
...the northern ripples have sucked with their frigid lips the traces of love.

By disappearing... these burning letters have mixed themselves within the
saltiness of things... and will return one day to you... Sidi Moussa.

Their memories will live near your exotic prickly pears... in a solar universe...
...that will offer to their souls an eternal intimacy...
        ...in the warm whiteness of your name.

Lovers' prayer to Sidi Moussa

AVENUE DES ROCHES

Return to Marseille

Not too far from the Corniche, clinging to her rocks,
Zigzagging with happiness, at the feet of the Bonne Mère,

Between the maritime pines and the urban cicadas
Among the hot white granite, color of snow, to come,

Exists a ball of yearn made of remembrances.

It began to wrap itself an Autumn day.

Under its cover, shades of lavender and of woolly substance,.
Was the fragility of images and sounds,
Brittle and tender.
As though time had imposed
A sacred and gentle envelope around them.
By protecting them against disappearance and neglect.

An Autumn day came, and between the night train to Paris,
And the New York boat for immigrants,

Between the kisses on the platform, made of moisture,
And the familiar faces disappearing in the mechanical vapor,
The Avenue des roches became smaller and smaller.

This Autumn day, upon leaving the proletarian Vieux Port,
With its precious and rotten smells of leftover fish,
Its faces burnt by the sea salt,

Upon the last sounds of the sounds
Of the fish market and floating debris,

I got dressed in my little immigrant suit,
And I went away.

I left behind the solar and Provencal chiaroscuro
Of the side streets of the Fort Notre-Dame neighborhood.

The paternal and solid sea bank of César, the wise father.
Of Fanny, the romantic and susceptible daughter.
And I went to pursuit the more adventurous,
But solitary, one of his son, Marius, to the New World.

I seem to have worn, as a shell, this little costume,
Like a last vestige of my past,
In order to protect myself of the New.

As shown by the triply well buttoned jacket
On a freshly taken snapshot on an American street.

The jacket has since disappeared in the trash heap of yearly growth.
And only the daily rites remained in the rites of our lives.

The Mediterranean soil, still attached to our soles,
Began to intermingle, by necessity, by habit,
With the frozen soil of the Labradorean present.

We had cut down, level to the ground,
Before leaving, and with good intentions,
Our fruit trees of remembrance.
All in the belief of helping them survive the anticipated cold.
And we forgot about them.

We forgot about them, until a Spring day of middle age.
A day empty and emptied of interest.

Empty and emptied of future ideas and possibilities;
But full of reflection upon our roots
And what these meant to us.

We had cut down, upon leaving,
And with good intentions,
The miniature rose bushes and the aromatic trees,
The date trees and the olive trees,
That we had found too heavy for the trip.

The Canebière and the rue de Rome,
The Cours Piette Puget and the Préfecture,
The afternoon swims at the Pointe Rouge,
The trips to l'Estaque,
Had shrunk so as to take as little space as possible in the suitcases.

And we fought, without much consciousness of it.
We fought against the invasion through the front door
And the non protective walls against the cold.

We fought to preserve a little of oneself.
A little of things that are now disappearing
Into the new language to learn and new ways to live.

We armed ourselves with fish soups and ratatouilles.
Facing off the neighborhood suspicions.

We opened in familial settings bottles of wine,
Facing off puritanical disapproval.

And we juggled as best we could the eclectic cultural balls.
Hoping to keep them in the air as long as possible,
And not appear ridiculous.

We will only rediscover this past, one day,
While walking and then tripping
Against this new greenish growth we had thought dead.

The ball of yarn will drop from our fingers
And unfurl.

And like these dehydrated substances that regain their initial forms with water,

All these images, all these sensations, all these moments
Will come back to life

Under the sky of remembrance,
Some evening on the Corniche,

As the Château d'If will begin to disappear in the Mist of the night.

SILENCE OF THE SOULS

The Kasbah across the street, the past behind.
The Ricard in the glasses and the nightmares in their thoughts.

Lives that had washed upon the wet sands of neighborhood rumors:
"No future... this woman...
...you know?
He beats her... they say."

The organized collective war had ended.
Not the intimate and hidden meanness.
"If the Germans come back...
...I'll have your husband arrested!"

Military housing
With prickly echoes heard in the hallways.

Behind prying grey window slats,
Other prying darker colored glances.

Filthy words of spouses toward other spouses
With detestable whispering flavors.
Nourished by the lack of food.
Enriched by the manure of wars of occupation.

The war is over
But not the doubts.
The war was gone, but not the ghostly shadows... of men...
Who hurt other men.

The sun of Provence had disappeared,
Hidden behind clouds made of the libelous commentaries
Of neighborhood women.
Of denunciations of brothers by brothers,
Leading to sadistic torture of rue Paradis in Marseille.

This beautiful sun, obscured by a blinding pain.
Descent into grief that takes away the will to breathe:
The only surviving family member shouting his anguish:
"Arrest me also, I, too, am a Jew!"

The prejudices between collaboration
And the black market tickets.
"Do you know what she did...
For a pound of sugar?"

The war came to its end...
But not the double cross and the dubious actions.

Past events in which existed a German machine-gun,
Whose apparition on a kitchen table,
Was the pride of the men of the family.

Its presence was explained by a stern motherly glance
And the father's silence.

Pasts where whispers of infidelity were heard,
The same thoughtlessly repeated.
Emotional blackmail, social and intimate leftovers
To which eternal worth was given.

The whole followed by an ultra human glance of sadness
In these otherwise smiling faces,
Whenever the 'little one' wanted to know...
"...Why?"

———————————————

And so, it's a dash toward the Maghreb:
Hoping to find, for one last time,
The fable exotic landscape that shows the soul and the memories
Comfortably nude... in the natural setting of things.
The pockets thus emptied of the spare change
Dirtied by the past.

Between the pastis and some patois accented jokes,
Two men find understanding and agreement
In a reciprocal fertile silence,
While nearby a little boy was playing
With the concrete innocence of white metal toy cars.

Much like an animal modifies its behavior
In proximity to mankind,
This youth had learned to instinctively respect,
And find natural this verbal void:
Otherwise confusing to other adults.

All of this with the background of intoxicated bees
Flying above the garden table
Under the eternally aromatic fig tree.

Beneath its large dark leaves
The few spoken words had the symbol

Of precious substances that make for the joy of men.

This silence alone could open these hearts made airtight
By the harmful noises of life.

Around this table were these two men:
So different one from the other.
Linked in a non-verbalized friendship.

Two men who had decided one day, to go fishing
On a piece of Africa
On the northern tip of Africa.

And to find in the silence of the hunt
For the illusive 'big' catch
The concrete happiness whispering in the Atlantic wind.

Of the killings, the cowardice and other things…
Remained only the bleeding scars
In their heart.

In front of me was left only the shell of their bodies
Reservoirs of all that.

Bodies containing only the left-over of happiness
To which they drank their Pastis.

And the pain that they attempted to melt
Under the North African heat, near the Kasbah of Salé.
Far from the Vieux Port.

Two Marseillais near the walls of the Kasbah.

BETWEEN THE HANDSOME SPAHI
AND THE LEATHER SATCHEL

Between the handsome Spahi,
In his limitless messianic landscape,
And the anonymous patient,
Immobilized prisoner, captured by plasticized tubing,
Unfurls what we call a life.

Between the primary red and blue of the cape draped over his horse,
And the toneless whitish color of the mortal hospital sheets,
We feel the need to believe that existence must have a goal.

Between the yellow dry heat of the Sahel,
And the frozen white streets of the Labrador,
The body cools down for all times surrounded by moist glances.

Between the handsome Spahi, on his horse…
Loyal by name… difficult and unruly,
Exists the other antithesis that too often fills and controls our lives.

These typical, daily, hidden lives do not carry the Embellishments of great
personalities.
Those decreed of noble heart and genealogy.

These great characters of society, found under dramatic lights.
Lives full of great gestures that seem to be eyeing themselves in mirrors.

While for the majority, our lives get lost in the ambient noise of neglect.
As they pass from stage left to stage right, in the black of a black backdrop.
Without approving glances, without encouragement, with no ovation.

In those lives, no found jewels, furniture and beautiful thoughts to fill the
museums of posterity.
In these anonymous lives are found more often anonymous children,
Abandoned religiously on the front steps of churches into the arms of others.

We give them names… gratuitous names…
Names found in Italian dictionaries…

Solitary

And we set them on their way
Towards their lives. Hoping for the best.

Yet, all we need is to find a morsel of humanity.

A morsel of universality, that Montaigne searched for,
With such optimism in each individual.

We only need to find these candelabras
From Hugo's *Misérables* that we all carry with us,
From obstacle to obstacle,
That define in our eyes... our own...
...as well as...
The goodness and beauty of others.

There are places in each of us, if we care to recognize them,
For this presence, this object, both inert and verbal.

He ended far from the disintegration of the warmth of his North African dream,
Far from the old leaky pipes of war time Marseille,
The streets were now snowed covered;
But his smile had remained sunny.

In spite of the inhumanity of war
He had kept his nickname of 'Gendarme Sourire.'

Behind the easy... too easy smile,
Exists this man who had known the happiness
That makes women happy.

And so here we are, going through the drawers of yesterday.
Looking to reconstruct, in his duality, the entirety of an entire man.

To reconstruct the man around the idealizing structure that is memory,
And to give him back his flesh, rich in contradictions and taboos.

We look for an object which could speak for the man
When his humanity, as well as family reunions,
Demand his presence.

On a garage shelf, in a corner of America,
In his 'eldorado' of the new world which had burned so long in his heart,
Far from the Basilica of his home town on top of the harbor of Marseille,
Not far from his street made famous by Pagnol,

On a wooden shelf, simple and unpainted,
Like a divine child in his divine manger,
Ended up his leather satchel.

Made of thick leather, coarse, almost crude of texture.
As though to differentiate itself from these luxurious leather goods.
Those you take to nights at the opera.

As though this satchel wanted, by its common appearance,
To pass incognito in the spaces of life.
As though this object, witness to history, had wanted to be Forgotten under its mean appearance.
That we would be mistaken as to what it had seen.

And so it came to be, that far from the insanity of the round ups of Jews,
Far from crying children in need of food,
This satchel came to rest in the American abundance.

It was his military satchel that had contained the illicit supplies
For these terrorized people hiding in the basement of a church.

Substance rendered sacred,
By the gesture, the place and the times.

It is the anchor that we all search for in our odysseys.
And that permits men who would judge us,
As we close one last time our eyes,

To put us rightly, in spite of our apparent insignificance and our weaknesses,
at the center of humanity.

For a foundling named 'Solitary.'

BETWEEN THE MOTHER HEN AND HER SON

Contradictions of the heart and mind
Live longer than they should.

Making that walk into the wall of reality
That much more painful.

It eventually happens. It must happen.
Carrying past symbols,
Metaphors of lost innocence,
In our neglected back pocket

Like marbles from our last elementary school game.
Now under the snapshots in shelved shoeboxes.
A disheveled teddy bear with missing arm.

Any symbolic leftover.
The death of someone. An animal.

A chicken maybe.

Disproportional amount of time invested.
Young chicks becoming part of our human family.

Then feathered family of proud mother hen:
No nonsense Cocotte,
And regal white rooster with crimson comb.

Human vigilance to protect brood
From perils of 'bled.'
From prey birds and vipers of the Maghreb

Microcosm of barnyard happiness.
Anchored in the unshakable solidity
Of its personal value.

North African seasons and years followed.
Dry cracked August mud
Overwhelming December grass

The animals had their habits:
Cooling Summer potatoes plant shade.
Back of cages in tropical rains

Noble chicken solemnity. Authenticity of the vision.
Taken, by me, as possession of the sight

Litany of loved images
Creating illusions of ownership
In a little boy's heart.

The day came and was told
That we were going away.
"That's the way the grown-up world is."

Red eyes and pieces of conversations
From behind closed doors.

I knew we were leaving
Yet I did not know.

Until the day, until the day
That they killed my rooster.

The one that had slept under my arms
In the warm African sun.
The one that had defended his family
Against all dangers.
The one I had decreed more solid
Than the hard North African soil.

This infamous couscous contained
More spirituality than the pathetic sermons
From our well meaning parish priest

In the long run, belief and authenticity
Are where truth imposes itself
On the common gestures of daily lives.

The son of Cocotte was dead in our plates.
No need to blaspheme:
It was not the Son of God

But I have had the nagging feeling,
Since that last meal,
That day in my youth,

That an essential part of my life
Had dissolved itself in front of my eyes.

So, between the white eggs of animal Genesis
And this couscous,
I accepted to eat this animal

Whose death encapsulated
That we can feast on earthly meals,

Yet be left with our eyes full of tears
And our stomachs empty and hungry.

(above) This photograph was taken in Salé, Morocco, circa 1950. My hair is short and my sister, Marie Louise, will be married shortly and go to America. You can feel the ever present sun in this picture.
(*Jean-Yves Solinga collection*)

CHAPTER 2

CITY OF LIGHT
CITY OF NIGHT

In this chapter the poems are essentially about the Paris of both, tourist postcards and hard reality. The city of happy eternal life and beautiful architecture. The city of boulevards, bistros and historic cemeteries.

It is a perfect backdrop for sitting down at the "movable feast" of Hemingway's fame. Being young or older in Paris is always special. It IS Paris!

Even waiting under the rain in "Au Départ de Saint Michel" unfurls a romanticized spectacle of iconic Métro entrances and insane traffic. Or seeing a corpse being pulled out of the Seine in front of the Louvre where there is a rich contradictory mixture of the physical beauty of the buildings and the lesson of this dead man as exemplified by the magic of the presence of a nearby nubile tourist.

With some inspiration from well-known French actors, singers and writers, this city stays eternal. The duality of the "tough guy" of French movies of my youth, Jean Gabin, who was like a love stricken school boy in the arms of Brigitte Bardot. The city made for lovers of Georges Brassens where the benches become as intimate as their own bedroom. The exotic eyes of the mesmerizing gypsy Esmelrada of Victor Hugo's *Notre Dame de Paris* through which we see the eternal fight between the sublime and corrupted: To see Paris again for the first time.

The Existentialist Paris of Jean-Paul Sartre, at Saint-Germain-des-Prés where this usually cold, atheistic and abstract philosopher is seen living through the Other who will succeed him. This is an invitation for that Other to, in turn, know the same moments in this city: "The "Others" Will Always Have Paris."

Paris is also a state of mind for the long run. One should know happiness "With or Without Paris," and be prepared for the reality of Paris after Paris: "Yin Yang in Paris." We are thus left with lyricism in trying to recreate it: "Not far from Père Lachaise," the famous cemetery of the famous, such as Jim Morrison: "To Live and Die in Paris."

WITH OR WITHOUT PARIS

It was not Paris… after all. Nor the plane trees, or the river banks.
It was not Rue des Rosiers. Nor the falafel.
Not the Marmottan, nor Monet. And especially not Clichy and its lubricity.

It was the breeze color of the desert.
This presence through the Egyptian cotton.
The immediacy of things and glances.

It was carnal and burning fulfillment
That had existed in their hearts
Well before the Medieval towers.

Well before Paris,
Paris was in them.
In spite of the ambient Labradorean cold.
The frigidity of a cafeteria.
In spite of societal taboos.

And then, the ultimate embrace,
Like all ultimate glances.
Everything will be contained in everything.

Everything will have been enunciated.
The terminal, feminine and labial vowels,
Will have been written.

Paris, is always for lovers…
As long as one of the two thinks about it.
Each in their own lives.

Once Paris,
One can delicately fold its images.
Put them… there, in a pocket.

They will crease themselves: chafing against reality.
But like Pascal's *Memorial*,
They will be safe in the lining of things.

One will eventually always be able, with trembling fingers,
To gently and tenderly find again this beautiful haunting glance
On the sidewalk of an eternal Parisian bistro,
Among the yellowing folds of a snapshot,
Imprinted on the soul.

YIN-YANG IN PARIS

The city revisited

From its square, Notre-Dame's own beauty caused him pain.
Superb words, full of narcissism come to his mind.
Like... sublime... grotesque...

All this is too easy.
Hugo would describe... while for him: it is in his blood.
He has absorbed the living dust of this city.

Now... alone with some sort of septicemia of the soul.
A blackish streak goes up his arm.
Like venomous stigmata, that, by their corporal presence
Symbolize hers... now missing.

Literary descriptions of Paris
Read in the protected comfort of his armchair.
Filtered smells of academia
Quietly tasted with approving head movements
Like an herbal tea
Healthy, light and transparent.

Literature is so beautiful!
Plastic-colored tears
Made of inert molecules.

But life...! His presence in front of those towers!
What does he do with them?
What does he do with all the remains?

He needs to shout...
A selfish cry... as he leans against this old wall,
Rue des Rosiers,
Where he disregards the anguish of this place:
Seeing instead his own.

Apparently, the memory of Things
Is no more than a very human way
To allow ourselves to suffer longer.

It is, after all, what he makes himself feel,
By the scraping of his elbow
Against the granite of the walls.

He should instead feel the infamy of this site:
The gratuitous denunciations, the decimated families.

While, instead, the self centered exclusivity of Love
Forces him to see only her face… her beautiful exotic glance
…and nothing else.

Enormous opposites ignore each other.
Presence and absence.
The warmth of her body and the coldness of his.

They more than ignore each other,
They murder one another with the zealot conviction that all religions
Have known throughout times.

For in his heart
Now exists the most dangerous of creeds…
…the one known by desperate hearts.
The very one that fills the minds with this inquisitional zeal.

He tortures himself on this site void of moments past.
Those, very much like the humid cocoon of her presence.

These same neighborhoods
Now, solidified, petrified.

Like a dog, with hungry eyes and an empty stomach
He sniffs around for smelly remnants
Of yesterday's falafel, once in her hands…
For her smiles and pregnant glances.

The cottony softness having now disappeared,
He is surrounded now by the rough stoniness of the sidewalks.

In the midst of the sweetness of the vision
Of a reciprocal and still steamy couscous.

THE "OTHERS" WILL ALWAYS HAVE PARIS

"Death [of the writer] became only a rite of passage and earthly immortality offered itself as a substitute for eternal life.... Dying within it [human kind], was to be born and become infinite but if one were to mention to me the hypothesis that a cataclysm could one day destroy the planet, even fifty thousand years from now, I would have panicked... I cannot think without fear about the cooling of the sun: that my contemporaries would forget about me upon my funeral, I don't care; as long as they survive me I will be among them... but were humanity itself to disappear, this would kill the dead for good."   Translated from Jean-Paul Sartre's autobiographical "Les Mots"

Distant and intimate.
The glance-passion of Hope
in this Other.

This Other, that we saw
in the hellish play of Sartre.

And yet,
Everything that surrounds them... will live again.
Through the instinctive common gesture of the instant.
Shimmering and full of humanism.

All of them, at first, without distinction.
But all, personal and precious
in the long term of memory.

This Other, will feel in turn in his arms
the shivers of ecstasy
in the flavor of the eternal moment.

Rue Saint Lazarre:
at the corner of the still warm croissant.
The daily gesture replayed for them.

The Paris of a couple at Saint Germain-des-Prés
who will kiss sensually one more time
in the spiritual silent glow of vocative candles.

From the Sacré Coeur, at midnight,
erasing their vision of a New York full of return trip,
the replica, below on the ground, of the night stars.

Place Blanche:
the sound and light show of the raw light bulbs of movie houses.
And the foretelling of the erotic essences of a coffeehouse baba-au-rhum.

The repeated wish of the Atheist:
that of choosing, of leaning, in the depth of time and words,

27

towards the idol worship of the ephemeral nature of a pastry.
Thus pushing back through the essences of evaporated alcohol
this question of life and death... of brutality and finality.

In a new exotic glance of exotic eyes:
in the sanctuary of the Everything of Every Things.
While a kiss gives once more to this Other
the burns of the original secular stigmata.

Beautiful intimate eyes:
that will see again the first moments in this instant to come...
an intimate future... removed from their own.

At Sidi Moussa:
Others will find themselves on the reddish rocks.
And everything will live again in the fragility of fragile glances.
In a perfection protected from Time.

The waters of the Labrador and those of the Maghreb,
will fertilize each other and for always,
next to the lustful poetic sounds of sensual labials and virile consonants.
Under the rhythm of the alternating flow of the waves.

On the lips:
color of heat and crimson, others will feel,
at a prosaic cafeteria table with sequestered odors,
offering a somber daily menu...
their stellar explosive moment face to face with Love
at the instant of molecular birth.

In the space of a dance, Another will be able to know,
during a few moments, the need and the exaltation to reconstruct in his arms
the presence of a woman vanished in the musical perfume.

Avenue de Clichy:
in the Paradise of a bedroom, another couple will know
the shivers of bodies under their sheets
where lust will multiply theirs.

And there, there...
This vision by Sartre... written as though by chance.
With a hint of the gratuitous.
A burning paragraph in the midst of an avalanche of rather frigid smart words.

A passage out of sync in this writer known for cold philosophical straight lines
and an unfortunately amphibian look.

Well... there,

he leaves us, humanists, and us humans.
He leaves us in our most beautifully biological weakness.
He leaves us facing the money that counts:
our spiritual solidarity in front of Things.

Facing the deaf solidity of Things.
He leaves us in this Parisian bed.
He allows us to see, in this happy couple,
the glance of victory of the real *prise de conscience*.

All of this,
outside of academic and philosophical platitudes.
There where it counts... the beads of sweat on their chests
and the closing of eyelids under reciprocal glances.

It is at the limit of temporal love that we meet this philosophical site.
We used to be afraid of this dry world, deadly to Mortals.
Where, turn into powder of stellar dust,
these temporary Lovers on the sandy beaches of Prévert.

It used to be only in the interspaces of literature
that existed a place where we could build our hopes.
And, after all, what is literature?
What is Art... Words?

It is the place loved by sickly writers.
By half-blind painters, by these beautiful spirits
to whom only a few days are left in order to capture her perfume.
And the way her eyes closed upon a kiss.

But all this exists in the reality of the untouchable.
And the impossible.

Until the day when the statement by this Other in the chance of a written passage,
Or facing this painting, this canvas in the corner of a museum.
He passes in front... with envy... and holding his breath.

The passing passion... now dissipated in Time.
The passion... felt by the artist at that instant,
In this subject of inspiration and desire now made eternal.
By the glance, the fervor.
Through the fortuitous presence of the Other.

The void of Atheism, it seems,
Fills up with the somewhat recalcitrant and chance presence
Of these Others who will follow us.
We are thus left with only the hope in this belief.

NOT FAR FROM PÈRE LACHAISE

Not far from Père Lachaise... not far from Things that speak of oblivion.
Not far from a solidified past... untouchable and unchanging.

Not far from Great Men who thought themselves greater.
Not far from Great Men who did not want to be forgotten...
        ...from Little Men... forgotten in their lifetimes.

Not far from classical cadavers... of Molière and Balzac fames...
And The One from across the Atlantic...

"Come on baby... light my fire."

Not far from respectful objects:
        ...such as a flower for Piaf.
And those symbolic:
        ...a yellow-hued condom... for Morrison.

Not far from pompous and tired monuments to the dead...
        ...to this Youth immobilized by battlefield trenches and by marble.
Not far from the powdered remains of soldiers...
        Those enveloped by a shroud made of the fiber of flags.

Upon leaving this place of cultural and obligatory pilgrimage...
        ...a place halfway between the disinterest of the Living...
        ...and the pride of the Dead...
His eyes focused on more mundane things...
        ...those of the moment.
That is to say: the ever-present danger of uneven cobblestones and dog dropping...
Reflecting upon the place and manner of his next meal...

        ...He saw the future...
He saw a parallel universe...
He saw what could never be...
He saw what would never be...
        ...what he could never have...

She was here...
        ...boyish hairstyle...
        ...dressed in black...
        ...slick colored pants...
        ...holding a little boy by the hand.

It was the future... constructed of a magic and idealized material...
A future made outside of the fragile solidity of burial stones...

...made of an immortal substance... even more durable...
...that of passion and love.

A future born of... and from... an enormous need to remake...
...the too repetitive present...
...and the too forbidden future.

Made of a substance of pure fantasy...
...that only the love of the impossible can produce and pursue.

Absorbed by this vision... he found himself in the center of the world...
...where... only things that matter can coexist:
...where Time and Space is for Others...
...where the Amoral and Happiness wink at each other...
...a place where decrepitude IS for Others...
...and immortality... for Them.

"Come on baby... light my fire."

While the sound of brakes and horns were trying to put him back into reality,
While the elbows of tourists wanted to put him back into his body,
...his glance was taking him out of Matter...
...yes... out of Things.

He was looking upon this spectacle... this apparition...
...through the eyes of Those that know nothing of Time...

Like a jaded god...
...playing with his unending and boring Hours...
He was seeing in this woman what his soul demanded of him...

...the mother of his child.

He recognized in her all that he thought he had left behind by coming to this
city of the moment... of the present.
And as he felt a lump in his dry throat...
...he recognized the hips... the curves... the walk...
...the overly high heels... according to his personal opinion...
...the dark glance... and the stern pout that defines the chic of Paris.

She was here... next to him... so he believed.

But Père Lachaise and his lessons were not very far away!
He could see now the real future...
...the one, that keeps us from restful sleep...
...the one that makes us fear losing happiness... while in the very

middle of it…
…the one that brings us to the saddest core of the human condition:

> …that is to say: the very consciousness of joy…
> …and the fear of living without it.

He could therefore see a future… but without him.

In this child lived the leftovers of himself…
…facing complete oblivion.

His monument was only made of only of the flesh... but it was enough.

To the song of Je manque de toi *by Blondin*

TO LIVE AND DIE IN PARIS

Reflecting upon a métro incident

Flashes of Sacré Coeur… stairs of stone, full at the top with a red-tiled sky.
Cosmopolitan shadows of plane trees, and narrow apéritif sidewalks.

Between métro stations… screeching…
…hearts stopping… just like their railcar.
Reflected echoes of quick sounds and glances, and shallow breaths.
City of light, darkened by an airless tunnel.

Between quick glances, lifetime of memories.
City of light and sensual hours coming to an end.
In this tunnel and would-be tomb.

To live or to die.
To die with her fingers intertwined in his.

To live or die is easy.
Longing glances taking them from nothing to the other side of nothingness.

In search of a better place and time.
To die or to live… what is the difference?

So Paris… it is… where their hearts and their bodies always will be.

To live and die in Paris…
Coming out of the tunnel… they'll live for another day.

Mere mortals… they have no choice in their deaths.
So, placidly they sit on their blue plastic seats.
A sliding métro door in charge of their future.

But what if…
…what if they could choose?
To have lived and to have died in Paris?
And letting things go?
And having no more to add?
Knowing that no more could be added?

With the only wish… just to let them die… and to have others continue on living.

Cultural boulevards, with sensual marble muses looking down.
Concentric arrondissements, full of the nuptials of different ethnicities.
Narcissistic bridges, looking with approval at their images in the water.
Old grayish stones and soft pâtisseries…
…all come crashing into an explosion of whispers and sighs.

Last visions of a last meal and last longing.
Flashes of curved Grecian columns and timid entrances under hellish gothic
portico scenes.

Stolen kisses in stolen time along the intimate shadows of side chapels.

False alarm, they'll live another day.
The question is… why?

Flashes of falafel and couscous burnt on the mind.
Liquid joy of vin gris from Meknès.
And the need to stay awake.

Damning sleep, because it is not living.
Instead, to stay awake… to make memories.

From atop Montmartre, late at night,
Flashes of your life go by.
Around with The Tower's beam.
And you wish that you could make a stand.

To make life stop right there and then,
For… to live and die in Paris…
…must be what paradise is all about.

City of light, city of night…
Where are you Jim?

Speak to us from Père Lachaise...
...did that work for you?

Chocolateries and history.
Elegance on heels and slim profiles.
This must be God's place for recreation,
...where the culinary IS religion

All around chaos... all around outside and beyond is death and destruction.
All around the wants and anger of things and people.
But in his hands... in the darkening darkness is the now and forever.

Flashes of all and eternity... flashes of all that ever will be.
Complete peace among complete agony and pain.

As so it is... and so it should be... and so it should have been...
That the last glance would be on and returned by the object of desire.

To live and die in Paris.

Afraid to sleep

Afraid to miss something...
Afraid to miss a minute of Happiness... he walks...

...He walks with a feminine glance...
...wanting to be possessed by the virile gentleness of the smells of the
Quartier Latin.
Intimacy rendered more pressing...
Intimacy rendered more exciting...
...by pushing it off... to a pregnant future...
...by asking...
"Do you want to talk about existentialism?"

Choices between the palpable human and the untouchable humanism...
...and to have a taste of both.

To live and die in Paris... for living after Paris is death.

Having seen the hard marbly sheen of the reality of tomorrow...

He'll live instead in the cottony softness of yesterday's walks...
...on the uneven hardness of the cobblestones along the Seine.

And thus live... and thus die... in Paris.

"AU DÉPART DE SAINT-MICHEL"

"Au Départ de Saint-Michel," next to a métro sign…
…we wait for the face with the features of happiness and the taste of hours to be.

Under the Parisian rain of the Latin streets… among the whistling tires…
…in the anonymous urban race…
…we wait in the wetness: seated nervously under the red sidewalk canvas
bending under the storm.

On the other side of the emotional doubts, that are becoming larger with
time… arrives, in silence, this animal at his feet.

A miserable mass of wet feathers…
…but an aggressive and inquisitive eye.

The left hand allows some croissant scales to drop…
…and he opted to see in the spectacle under the table… a backward glance
of gratitude.

He wanted to see a comrade in this gray mass jumping among this abundance.

Under these magic Manna flakes was taking place an important animal scene.

He wanted to read, in this nervous glance, a silent note of appreciation.

This symbiotic animal made him enter in his world…
without gamesmanship… without pretense…
…for they were fulfilling, at this particular time, a space in each other's lives.

And amidst the scaly flakes of croissant…
  This particular day under the rain…

We learn, once again, the lesson…
  Known to Sisyphus at the summit…

Of the equivalence in front of the world…
  Between the weight of our biggest anguish…

And that of the nature of the substance in the beak of a bird…
  Lost in the rain.

BETWEEN L'ÎLE DE LA CITÉ AND L'ÎLE SAINT LOUIS

Between L'île de la Cité and L'île Saint Louis lives a kiss.
It is found nestled in a French style short black hair... full of the smell of love and virility.

It happened following a quick turn of the head over the left shoulder...
    ...toward the lips of desire...
...having wanted to just see again, respectfully, the flying buttresses and the monument to the deportation...

    ...and... love remade the city in its own image.

This is a miraculous kiss made up of unrelated pieces.
It is made up of 'falafel' with the smells of an oasis at sunset... and of languorous couscous... that transport them to a warm North African night... in white cotton... under naked and sensual strings of electric light bulbs.

It is made of the silence of two souls surrounded by the shouts of the joy of children on the uneven stones of the banks of the Seine with its reflections of a Gothic rosace.

It is made of this unfortunately too human mixture for the thirst of eternal voluptuousness... among the temporal grayishness waiting for them in a return trip in an airline terminal.

It is made up of earthly happiness... measured in seconds... just by seeing a limitless and smiling glance...
...among the urban fatigue...
...seated on a blue folding chair in a subway from Dante.

    ...and especially... just by seeing for the first time an "Impression, soleil levant"...
...and ironically... making of beauty... the source of stigmata of the void in the future.

In the middle of this doubly consecrated site to beauty and suffering...
...lives this kiss.

Between L'île de la Cité and L'île Saint Louis a couple is embracing on a bridge.

All that is left of this couple are images rendered transparent and fragile by society and its laws.

This kiss lives in the glance of an accidental driver who witnessed it... and

…that same night, a woman came to know a renewed passion in his arms.

A fertility flowed under this bridge among the stones raised in the name of thousand years old sleepy and touristy gods.

An eternal goodness flowed from this couple among this symbol to denunciation and religious evil.

Among this traffic with envious eyes… a gentle authentic, peaceful and refreshing mist floated around this statuesque and solid couple.

Between L'île de la Cité and L'île Saint Louis exists a kiss.

At Saint Germain-des-Près burns a magic candle.

It burns in a church with wooden beams blackened by years.
It is at the cold and dead marble feet of an anonymous saint with distant eyes.

At Saint-Germain-des-Prés burns a magic candle… with an eternal wax.

The old women whisper about it from ear to ear.

They come to sensually touch it with their fingers twisted by the years.
They come to look at it with their washed-out eyes.

"It is the candle of the atheist and the young woman… the ones kissing and crying," they keep repeating.

They all move away with a carnal smile, which hides a newfound lubricity.

This magic candle brings back up a blaspheming sap in these bodies forgotten by men and years.

In Saint Germain-des-Près burns a magic candle…
…the one of eternal human passion.

And like these sterile women who call upon your name…
          …Sidi Moussa…
…among the litanies of sighs coming from the old, dry, cracking, wood seats…
…they rub this candle wishing for their old youthful passion… and their first kiss behind a door.

This, indeed, is the arrogance of Love…
          …the innocent selfishness of Love…

how... with a contagious fever...
>...to make of Paris a private and nuptial place...

...like a bedroom with draped light... where only the glance of anticipated desire exists.

It is then that he becomes aware... upon seeing this glance that demands an answer for its anguish about the future...

>...that God... it is true... created the world in seven days. And having done the same, all that will remain for them... of their universe...
>...will be the magic and immortality of this week.

A Biblical Genesis in Paris

TO SEE PARIS AGAIN... FOR THE FIRST TIME

Under the Parisian rain of an eternal Verlaine...
...between the sink and the closet...
>...amidst the ambient and much too intimate noises...
>...under the wavy and nuptial sheets...
...Paris remakes itself...
>...Paris recreates itself in the new passion...
>...of a new glance upon Things.

At the top of a circular stairway... in the film noir fashion...
...behind the building façade... with a Jean Gabin look...
...between Chic Boulevard and Alley of Desires...
...one finds again this passion among the wrinkles.

The thick and historic stones melt... in the fashion of Dali...
...under the warmth of the whispers of her words.
And the reddish lacework showing through the towers of Notre-Dame is a
perverted foretaste of Human duality.

The desire in her exotic eyes puts Esmeralda back in the center of the sacred
church square... still unquenched with sensuality.

He notices... for the first time... and without shame...
...that the fragile and virginal whiteness of Montmartre...
        ...is like hers... and had been like hers always.

On the benches made of Brassens-like wood... eternal lovers gaze eternally
upon each other...
...and... according to very earthly laws...

...those of the romantic cycle of the renewal of the plane trees...
        ...those of the smells of the chestnut carts under the electric
        light bulbs...
                ...those of the nearly Roman... uneven steps... leading
                to the Seine...

        ...nothing will stop them or forget them.

Between the twelve and twelve B is found the blue and white enameled plaque...
...that of desire and happiness...
        ...the very one that knows nothing of the future and the bills to pay...

        ...only the immediate minutes.

A door opens on a hallway licked by the years.
A rusted bell buzzer leads to a place that refuses to age...

        ...that of Lovers.

And suddenly... among all this beauty of a setting sun reflecting into an
oblique mirror...
        ...this city... previously beyond mere words...

                ...allows itself to be gently captured by the architecture of
                their bodies.

A contemporary look at Victor Hugo's Notre Dame de Paris.

WE WILL NOT ALWAYS HAVE PARIS

When the last cosmonaut... on the last ship...
     ...leaving the orphaned earth... turns around...
     ...he will see crystallized silicon on the way to a little mound of dirt.

He will see lumps of anonymous rocks in anonymous order...
     ...all that will be left of the elegance of the Champs-Élysées...
     ...all that will remain of the neoclassical majesty of the Arc de Triomphe.

The mortal remains of an immortal city.

One last glance towards a reddish dirt... inhabitable wastelands...
     ...once the site of Holy Shrines...
     ...of powerful men... giving powerful speeches.

One last glance... upon dusty artificial lines...
     ...once worthy of mindless violence and hatred.
One last echo of dying words...
     ...about man's dominion over things and beasts.
One last somber thought...
     ...about the ephemeral nature of eternal beauty.
One last reflection...
     ...about the arrogance of illusion and delusion of humanism over matter.

As man departs the dying solar system...
     ...he will... for the first time since Galileo...
     ...be truly put in his place.

Nowhere... in the middle of nothingness.

In the corridors of the space ship will be heard the beginnings...
     ...of cries of envy and jealousy.

As Sartre had predicted:
Hell will... indeed... be... other people.

For...
...along for the ride...
     ...man will have brought with him... in his precious luggage...
...not only his finest linen...
     ...but also... his darkest...
          ...blood-incrusted remnants...

          ...from the depth of his closet.

Cain's descendants in space

BETWEEN LIFE AND THE CORPSE

Paris, city of life:

Upon my leaving you
I saw,
Saw, next to your prestigious Louvre,

Next to your many bridges,
On the walk for your lovers,

A dead body on the ground.

The circle is closed.

Paris,

I saw,
Continuing my walk
On trembling legs,

I saw, leaning,
Leaning towards a lithography,

A pretty girl,
Offering me the sight,
The sight of shapely thighs.

The dead man is gone.

The circle is closed

(above) This was taken in Marseille, France, in 1952, during on of our many trips to visit family. My brother Pierre, me, and my father.
(Jean-Yves Solinga collection)

CHAPTER 3

SPLINTERED

This chapter is about the unstoppable need to make sense of things and people. If only we could leave our memory and our culpability at the door, or in a shoebox: quietly forgotten.

But instead, years into adulthood, we see the same truck that we did not get for Christmas because our father wanted to teach us a lesson in humility: "In Search of Blue and Orange." We then put this "little truck" on the mantel piece like Jean Valjean, of the *Misérables*, his candelabras. We feel guilty about the way we treated people who genuinely loved us: "Was it Roxanne or Hoxane? "

Or we see our "little girl" leave home to follow her destiny: "Between the Butterfly and the beautiful glance," leaving us with the mosaic of memories.

The up close fragile imagery of the color of lavender plants is used in "Lavender and Happiness" as a metaphor for that unease in front of what we know to be the ephemeral quality of joy and beauty. The stubborn dead leaf in the middle of the snows of February "Of Better Summer Hours" reinforces this feeling: poets torture themselves thinking of summer in a snow storm.

In some practical way, the very existence of all my lyrical prose is found in "For an Art and an Artist with no Goal." For it is in the very pursuit to recapture these disappearing images in Time, that words are put on the page.

This is a chapter about the hidden beauty of things and people around us and the resulting world of images if we take the time to recognize it. If not, it is "Silence: the Face of anti-lyricism." A void on the page is what is left of Time if art does not fight to fill it.

SPLINTERED HEART

Near the Temple of Baudelaire

It is upon breaking... against the glacial earth of the present...
...that the heart reminds us that he is still near.
Warm and steamy... he was still pumping... with timidity...
        ...and not knowing exactly why... by sheer habit...
...the still fluid remains of lubricity... cooled off by human laws.

We... we had tried to forget him... and be forgotten by him...
...in some dusty and quiet corner... of our life.

Finding ourselves progressively at ease in our daily routine filled with stupor
and middle-class yawning...
        ...but ...he... was still near.
Waiting for us to recognize him for what he is...
...what he was...
        ...the witness to our most splendid hours...
            ...and now... here he is...
...splintered into infinite shining and sharp scaly pieces...
...on a dirt floor that knows nothing of his worth.
We learn... then... that upon breaking...
...the heart recreates... with a knowing faithfulness...
...the first clouds to escape from the incense holder hiding the scent of Happiness:

... the sound of her eyelashes closing upon a kiss...

And we... who thought him to be asleep... dead of boredom...
        ...blind... and deaf!

It is upon breaking that the heart releases the vapors within...
...those of the first time...
        ...those of the first glance upon the blood red lips...
            ...and the virile abandonment to the call of the wild.

We begin to fill the void left by the object of desire...
...we fill the hole... with the debris of the leftovers of our lives.
In it, we throw precious whispers... adored smells... and bedroom eyes full of virility.

Enveloped by a sticky veil that stifles the future...
...blasphemous thoughts form in our silent and solitary mind.
Dark thoughts... in the darkness of darkness...
It is in this place full of temptations and possibilities...
...that we humble ourselves on the floor... in front of our divinities...
Naked and with no dignity... we are ready to offer anything.

It is at these moments that Humanity must have felt the need to invent...
...the concept of Good... the unreal... the surreal... Santa Claus... anything...
.   ...in order to quiet the painful crisis...
        ...at the sight of a dying father on a rented hospital bed...

        ...or that of a vanished sister soul...
        ...now somewhere else in the anonymous crowd of another life...

We catch ourselves pointing an accusing finger toward the gods...
...so great is the pain... gratuitous the injustice...
        ...and the object... precious.

Having built our gods from the mud of our weaknesses...
We look with astonishment upon their feet melting under the mist of our tears.
From the depth of our religious void... we cry for having lost her.
This object of our desire that had brought us so close to the Heavens.
This Soul... this Being... which by its very earthly carnal worth...
...had us taste the vaporous and transparent foods of the gods.

Like an old parish priest... discouraged at the sight of innocent dying children...
...we bow our heads in front of our wooden and ivory Christ...
...hanging... full of smoke under the transept of a country church.

It is at this precise moment that we invent what will save us...
                ...Evil.

It is at this precise moment... that we repeat in turn... the infamous Faustian oath...
...to whomever will put her back in our life.

It is then... that... still and unfortunately alone... under the sacred arches...
...and far from the pagan Proustian perfumes that had put her in our arms...
It is then... that coming back to earth... we leave... like the Christ of Vigny...
...this place full of creaking sounds and ancient mute stones.
We follow... full of guilt... the cold walls... and we exit.

Outside... in the world of Things... we nourish ourselves with echoes of the past.

A beautiful black butterfly zigzags in the solar syntax.
We start to fill the corporal void with the conditional and with suppositions:
...we should have... we could have...

And we begin to soothe with words... only words... the wounds received from the Stigmata of Love.

And man invented Evil

RETURNING HOME

If returning home... is seeing old places we saw when we were young...
If returning home... is hearing the rumble of an antiquated balance bridge...
If returning home... is feeling the wind shift from Eastern Point...
...and the New England fog rolling off the Mystic River...
    ...then we can... indeed... go home again.

If walking down some anonymous city street...
...you see a picture in a window of an English Springer Spaniel...
    ...and if you want to yell and embrace it at the same time...
    ...then you are home again.

If later in your busy life you hear yourself telling stories...
...of a slower and routine life...
    ...of blessed boring hours with nothing to do...
    ...of family anecdotes of disastrous Disney trips...
    ...then you are home again.

If the sight of common farm animals...
...endless winding... dark and rainy roads...
    ...bring a smile to your lips...

If meaningless arguments with your boss...
...remind you of... now... precious sibling fights...

If your first bite into a moist Danish reminds you of Gulino's
You will have gone...
...for having left it too soon...
    ...where all of us want to return as adults...
    ...you will have gone home again.

Advice to grown children upon leaving home

IN SEARCH OF BLUE AND ORANGE

On a chimney mantle exists a toy:
It is made of remembrance and wisdom.

A little truck, it would seem
Made of some common metal.

It is painted with a washed-out blue and orange
The effects of time and the fingers of an unknown child.

This obsolete truck bypassed by the years and technology is here,
Dressed in its most beautiful anachronism,
In the middle of aromatic candles and family pictures.

In the past exists a Christmas.
It is made of the too easy pleasures and ease of a child.
It is made of the disdain for those who have nothing
That only physical comfort can teach to us.

In this Christmas exists a toy store.
It lives on the corner of a street long gone in the past.

It is made of holiday shimmer and lights
Those help the child to easily forget the message of a couple
Unfortunately much realistic
Even for the agnostics.

A couple that had only the breath of tired cattle to keep warm their newborn.
It is made of things that allow us to believe that all is well
In a Universe where men do not love each other enough
And where children cry too often.

In this past exists a father.
The sadness and catastrophes of wars had marked him with their stigmata
That wound more deeply than the iron reddened by the flame

For, this sadness stays on the heart
While the others disappear in Time

Nothing is well on the Earth
After the nightmares of the gratuitous and useless death of the pages of history.

This past Christmas is made of envy and certitude in the eyes of the child.
In it, one only knows comfort
The one that lives in quiet forgetfulness

The one of the Middle class conscience
Face to face with the human insanities of the past and future.

It is made of the forgetfulness...
...The forgetfulness of things that count
Forgetfulness of the knowledge of what it is to want... and not have.
Forgetfulness of not having what we want most of all in the World
This blue and orange truck on the glass shelf.

This truck lives today on my chimney mantle.
After years of absence.
It came back into my life... in a chance encounter on a walk in Montmartre.

The man that I had become
Saw again in the display window... the colors for which he was searching...
In his heart... and in the endless meanders of life.

He had been searching, unknown to him, for
The colors of wisdom

The truck that my father had refused to give me:
"To teach you a lesson,"
...was often, over the years, told to me by my mother.

LAVENDER AND HAPPINESS

Electric blue Provencal landscape

Some things exist... to be put under our glance by the universe.
These things talk to us about what is important:
      ...ephemeral happiness.

The color of lavender fields is one of them.
The antithetical... understated beauty...
      ...of a gentle metallic blue...
      ...stops us in our mindless... repetitive... aimless walk.
We are irresistibly pulled toward this unreal presence...
      ...that contradicts the sterile surrounding dryness.

We approach this object of desire.

Like many visual human reactions, we want to contain it...
...to pull it to us...
      ...to fill our hands with it...
         ...and to rub it under our nostrils.

To feel ourselves satiated with this substance...
that yet... escapes from us as we near it.

And like Camus' Adulterous wife it is no less than a quasi-sensual...
intimate ceremony that awaits us.

But as in many privileged emotions within the experiences of things earthly...
...this one also disappears into time...
      ...as well as from our trembling hands...
      ...so that we are left with only the passion to reconstruct it...
         ...and the hope of a future happiness to see it again.

To the sound of "Douce France" by Charles Trénet

GHOSTS OF REALITY

Youth came back today... in brown eyes.
A hard... dark... look of coincidence.
Looking into me... through my surprise...
It's her!...

Knots of fear... as fresh as yesterday's.
Bursts of love as forceful as my souvenirs.
Cries of jealousy as loud as the last fight

Yesterday is long ago
Remembrance is weak... the will is strong
It's not her!...

Strange how what is not... can still be.
Inventing realities from pieces in our mind.
Resulting puzzle... truer in its fantasy...
Than the bag of groceries in my hands.

Pangs of the memories of love in a grocery store

MORE OR LESS GUILTY

The conscience of an Atheist

Feeling guilty... we try to judge...
     ...to rationalize the distance between good and evil.

We hear amidst... and in spite of the sighs in front of our face...
...the remnants of the echoes of a catechism found in a precious white church
full of the warmth of youth...
          ...and yet... forgotten long ago.
We awaken surrounded by the sulfurous clouds of our soul... dead for most
of the past...

                    ...while our body... full of life... is so happy... so happy.

It becomes difficult to deny to our fingers... what our fingers demand.
That which... in the sticky... silty...
     ...but warm matter...
...gives them a reason for being.

The joys of the moment... impose reddish and especially opaque colors...
...on the sinful stains.

Far from thinking of the salvation of the soul...
...we think rather of the enormous equation... this one...
...very personal and material...
...that reduces... all values...
               ...in all places...
               ...in all times...
                         ...to just this glance...
...the one perceived in the rays allowed by the curtains.

Through half-closed lids, the heat of the sheets becomes the one of deserts
where availability is at ease in its nudity.

Tripping on the red hot grains of the dunes creaking with dryness...
...the lips are looking for humidity that brings back life.

In the mirror, we cannot recognize any longer this person... source of evil.
Accusing voices talk of hedonism without redemption.

We then turn back... toward this other tabernacle...
...and we repeat the Lovers' Creed...

          "...We have to believe that Hell is full of happy people!"

51

BETWEEN THE BUTTERFLY AND THE BEAUTIFUL GLANCE

Entre le papillon et les beaux yeux

A last look... a last glance in the rear mirror...
...a diminutive elementary school...
...sun glasses from Montmartre...
...a box full of purses...
...an assortment of eclectic shoes...

Tangible things that we hold dear...
...in the closets of youth...
...because with their now empty playground and cheap plasticity...
...they remain precious pieces of *Her*...

And like our image of *Her*...
...we have decreed long ago...
...in our hearts...
                    ...that these... would never change.

Hurried hours... office hours... anonymous hallways...
              ...in anonymous emergencies...
...blurring into fading... and surprisingly... gentle memories.

All... transformed...
...concentrated...
...by the evaporation of time...
...under the warmth of unconditional parental Love...
...into perfect... precious... moments...
...of what lies between youth and adulthood.

A last look...
...a last glance...
...into what defines *Her*.

———————————————————

Wisdom is knowing when one is looking at it.

It came in a package from California:
...cocoons of future and beautiful butterflies...
...it said on the side of the box.

Another project... another piece of clutter on the nightstand.

From underneath the translucent mesh...
...would eventually emerge...

…what is too rarely…

…authentic and miraculous…

…amidst the other clutter…

…the one we call our daily lives…

…a miniscule-brained animal…

…a deformed… ugly butterfly… destined for death.

A Quasimodo looking up… this time… to His dark eyed Esmeralda.

Seemingly intelligently waiting for her daily return from school…

…he would exclusively seek out Her sugar-moistened finger.

There is still pathos and humanism in this scene…

…for it puts *Her*…

…like *Her* Grammy…

…Spiritually at ease…

…in the center of things…

Which often try to speak to us…

…if we know how to listen…

…in the language of the muted vibrations of a butterfly's wings.

A young girl, a butterfly and life.

BEATS OF THE UNIVERSE: A HUMANIST'S VIEW

Night stars, shining for nothing
Were it not for man's looking.

A setting sun, redoing eons old ritual
Older than man's arrival.
Spectacle with no romance
Without man's glance.

Crystals of water
Giving snow cover,
To wind swept hills:
For nothing
Were it not for man's reflection
On countless explosions.

Bursts of light
Taking metaphoric flight.

Though nature will follow its course
Without man as its source
An empty forest
Is only sterile rest

There is nothing inherently beautiful about the Universe.

OF BETTER SUMMER HOURS

Whirling dry leaf, released by the snow.
Solitary remnant of dying life.

Holding within your creases
Vague images of suffocating heat.

Daughter of green tribe,
You danced in the Summer's rays.

You now swirl alone.

Guided by a February wind,
Of what specific tragedy
Are you the example and moral?

Your sisters have long since been buried
Yet here you are still.

With brittle veins, looking for rest
This world is not for you
With your brown color in this strange whiteness.

So far up high and proud in yesterday's warmth,
Skeletal and prodigal you attempt to hide.

Don't envy me, though, behind my window,
Having myself only an electric sun,

Regretting like you, my better Summer Hours.

WAS IT ROXANNE OR HOXANE?

Was it Roxanne or Hoxane?

Girl of Life, and not of the convenience.

So what to do with her?

Blond sister of a friend.

Girl of coincidence,

Met by chance for a lunch date.

What dust in my eyes!

And yet! I was able to see her!

Wrongly read her soul.

I see her better now.

She's not here any longer.

FOR AN ART AND AN ARTIST WITH NO GOAL.
...EXCEPT: ART

We glance more and more behind us:
In order to extract wisdom?
Learn a lesson?
Build a guiding morale?

No, rather to search for a vanished 'me.'
What we know to have lost now,
What we did not know how to keep then.

The goal is inaccessible:
Remains only the exaltation of the pursuit.

SILENCE: THE FACE OF ANTI LYRICISM

His thoughts seemed to be lacking oxygen.
Ignored and dying as orphans.
He had no use for them.

Words themselves... feelings... made him nauseous.
Poetic prose, phonetic symbiosis,
Architectural mosaic inlaid into the cadence of syllables,
The gentle plasticity of vowels,
The beauty of the moment stopped in the moment.
Everything in everything seemed to be void of its meaning.

Noticing an element of weakness in the creative act,
Shame overtook him.

Instead of words finding echoes in each other,
Words were hurling past each other.
While in the past a magical cross fertilization
Would have taken place in the glorious mixture of imagery and ideas,
There existed now a disgust and fear of opening himself.

Their mutual voices seemed tired.
They had lost their intonation that had pleased him so.

Looking, now, for elements of happiness in their conversation,
Looking for a secret note that in the past
Would have made him hear and wait for the future.

He found only the neutral sterility of a reciprocal awkwardness.

And at the end... the pain,
The pain of having nothing to add:

> "I don't know how to finish this conversation."

Sterile ending, full of terminal words.
Sentences full of modifiers that cause fear in one's heart,
Instilling dread of love, of friendship, of tomorrow.

Antiseptic telephone conversation.
Ambience of an automobile, with colors of a parking lot.
Oppressive city air and summer heat.
Stifling metaphors for their last moments.
All his illusions had melted

Under the attacks of reality.
Her words were pushing him away from happiness.
Word after word, sound after sound, cadence after cadence.

Her words, so precious to him in the past,
Were destroying one by one his illusions.

Only an arid nervous laughter came out of his lips,
And then…

"I don't know how to finish this conversation."

That is when he discovered a hatred for his own sentences:
Haphazardly spread on yesterday's paper.

They all had been the result of a quasi-physical relationship
Between the mind, the fingers and the text.

These objects, these phonemes, had so well solidified his ephemeral states
of being.
The very materiality of words that brought so much joy in the past.
These words, he missed this day.

"I don't know how to finish this conversation."

And yet, he had known so well how to use them as
Heavy boulders,
Thrown into the temporal liquid to make of them Unmovable obstacles against
neglect.

Phonetic boulders, that would define,
By their very volume, well after his death,
What he had heard, seen, and touched.
What had touched him.

It was this very fertile antithesis
Between the physical, tactile, presence
Of the world on the page,
And that of the noise of souls brushing against each other.

Things that his poetic prose had wanted to capture;
But that now was scaring him.

He felt the overwhelming perversion

To erase what he had said.
From fear he would start believing in it:
Still or anew.
These very words that had allowed him
To exist in a parallel universe.

These words, in a privileged place, private and hidden,
A place of peaceful dédoublement, with no complex,
Where he could, as he wished, be this Other.

Far from the bills to pay.
Deaf, and especially, protected from
The moralizing of social duties.

Facing the eternal consciousness of an eternal darkness,
The human spirit pushes back this inevitable silence
With thoughts from Pascal.

Our Thinking Reed, facing the enormity of unthinking things, marches on.
It marches on, through, in various forms.

Such as… tortured musical notes on wrinkled paper.
A formula, an equation, an idea.
Imposing order on Things.

It marches on facing the humid wall of a cave.
Facing a scroll, the cellulose of paper.
Facing the electronic screen.
Facing tomorrow's technology,
That, like today, will allow us to stop the passage of time
Over the future love in future times.

The eye and glance will always question Things
And the very images that they impose on us

It is in from our very splendid human arrogance
That our pride will make us believe that
We understand.

It is there, that a fear, an anguish, a need,
Both selfish and generous
Run throughout the body, the mind.

There, that a force, at times irresistible,
Destructive at times, always fertile,
Will makes us set the Moment, with the sticky mud of passion,

on the walls of this cave.

It is this mud that will stop the present
As it stops running down the wet wall.
The way that we purposely put on paper
What we fear of just leaving behind
On the fragile surface of our thoughts.

Thanks to words, we know the greatest of privileges:
The dispensation given to the Muses:

To be able to lie openly.
To believe in the very illusions that we construct
Of tomorrow, of our happiness, of the future of our work.

"I don't know how to finish this conversation."

This might be the ultimate and true generous act of the artist:

To create, in the midst of poetic asphyxia, and from emotional bile,
A testament hoping to find in its future a sister soul

That will cry in its name.

(above) Class picture of my last year in Morocco 1959. At the Lycée Aldelmalek Al Saadi of Kénitra. I am in the third row from the front and the fourth from the right. To my right is Jean Russo behind whom I would run for my life while he would 'open' my way in rugby. We all knew that we would lose track of most of each other as our families made plans for their future departures. I was told it would be easier not to mention my leaving for America. To this day, I think it shows in the picture.
(Jean-Yves Solinga collection)

CHAPTER 4

DAYDREAM

Daydream, shows that even poets cannot escape some reality. The ugliness of reality. Overpopulation, social injustice, mindless organized killing, and so on.

In the poem "Daydream," we have this slightly flawed man who wants to deal with the different parts of his uneven daily life only to be stopped by his death in the Twin Towers.

Then there is the organized killing of all sorts: The religious, in "Mary Magdalene," where we see a woman who just wants to live her life with the man she loves. This vision is inspired by a powerful passage by the poet Alfred de Vigny who describes the human side of the struggle of the Mont of Olives.

The patriotic, in "Song of War," "I fantasize being six feet" and "The Sheets have to be cleaned," is where humans leave their humanity at the door and jump head first into glorified mayhem.

Then there is the cataclysmic in "Mankind and its Place" where inspired by Voltaire's account of the Earthquake of Lisbon, we see life slipping off the mud of happenstance.

There are the unrecognized daily heroes that change lives for the better, "Of Law, Justice and True Heroes." Men and women who do not follow blindly the codes written in the abstraction of a committee vote. They see a potential personal injustice. Not only do they prevent it; but make for a better future by their own decisions.

The reality of urban decay in "Empty Walk" where the presence of a family of pigeons in these rainy, empty streets make the absence of human families that much more painful.

The impending global threat of uncontrolled human growth in "Protoplasm." And yet, there is a happy, optimistic medium: "Between Science and Humanism," an ode to reconciliation between the apparently contradictory worlds in Academia, the hard reality of Science and the gentleness of the Humanities.

Hopefully, like the *Flowers of Evil* did for Baudelaire, maybe some beauty will nevertheless be found in all this reality.

DAYDREAM

Nothing like the blankness of a "severe blue sky,"
To paraphrase a CBS radio anchor,
For making it easier to sculpt any vision you want upon it.

From the top of the city,
Space became the fantasy of kindergarten clay.
It was malleable into any craving he wanted.

Voids and fulfillments in his life
Seemed to be hedonistically appeased
And egoistically savored.

Shortcomings, envies and needs,
Existentially fertilized each other,
into a happy, pregnant and seemingly endless future.

His gentle wife with the prairie-green eyes,
diplomatically distracted from any complicated or substantive discussion,
as she ate her cereal this morning.

Amazingly studious and respectful teenage children,
left watching reruns of the metaphorically pastoral
and innocent world of the Waltons.

The dark eyed friend on the next floor,
had once more sacrificed pieces of her soul and embers of her heart,
by offering precious moments to him.

Guilt and happiness had learned to co-exist,
in his biologically and emotionally aging heart.
Things were a happy shade of gray in his mind…

But, maybe… he should do something to elevate
what his loved ones… and those who loved him…
would think… in case… just in case…

When he again looked over his right shoulder,
away from the artificial blue of the computer screen,
toward peaceful natural azure and momentary escape…
only to see the nose of a plane…
…outside of the window…

Kiss the ones you love:
Deconstruction of a very blessed and slightly flawed man in the Twin Towers on September 11.

EMPTY WALK

Spaced… drops of fine rain.
Echoes of echoes of silent walls.
A wayward abandoned blue plastic chair.

Quick, fearful, instinctive look back:
Prevention from perceived foot steps.

Sad leftovers of Christmas lights.
Dripping sheet rocks and loose bricks.

Unused crosswalks and lonely green lights:
Priority to phantoms.

Beading drops on leather jacket skin.
Seemingly feeding moisture to denatured life.

Flashbacks of activities and heartbeats.
Once dignified doorways
Of dentists and CPA's,
Leading to cracked marble floors:
Reflecting cloudy decay.

Boarded windows
Hiding financial shame,
Away from today's latest
Economic global fame.

Urban renewal and social engineering.
'Benign neglect' and changing times.

Once powerful, beautiful city:
Tree lined and Greek revival.

Captains with untold wealth,
Made of the oil from speared whales.

The whole street now the recipient
Of reverse and still unguided mercantilism.

No one left to complain
In this cliché of a "gloomy and rainy night;"
But a family of pigeons
Rustling in the dark.

Once upon an inner city walk

THE SHEETS HAVE TO BE CLEANED

It started to be ingrained into women's brains
When running through and away
From the primordial muds
Of the muds of historic battles.

It started to be ingrained into women's brains
That the children
At their bloated and bleeding breasts
Had to be fed.

Men in their collective and rightful needs
Were of one mind.
To very purposefully maim
Or be stoically killed,

For that preferable patch of green.
That luscious river bank, that page of history.
That particular brand of true belief.

Blood had to be spilled.
Infidels properly sent to their respective gods.

Other worthless women and off springs
Had to be the inconvenient loss
Of the wrong side of History.

Protective walls and killing machines had to be invented.
Oceans crossed, autonomous people
Conquered, sternly civilized.

But for the women... for the women...
...The children had to be clothed and fed.

So it is with quasi-religious essence
Of what is right and proper
In the family of man,

With infinitely deeper value
Than soft oils on grandiose museum paintings,
With more dignity than sterile patriotic ceremonies,

That this woman in the midst of destruction and cries,
During a lull in confusion and flight,
Decided to deploy the flag

Of true sanity and deep humanity,

By hanging her clothes to dry
When the bullets stopped flying.

She then sat down on a shaky wooden stool
Next to a fire made of broken wood
Of her parents' bedroom furniture
To begin the evening meal,

With gestures that Rembrandt
Would not have dared feel worthy to capture.

Inspired by NPR interview of a writer who described a lull in fighting during which a woman took advantage by hanging out her wash. Also, Rembrandt' 'Supper at Emmaus.' The quiet dignity of common gestures.

ATTACK THE MACHINE

Spew it out from your guts... put it up on the walls of society
Scrawl it over the slogans and paper thin plasma images
Insert it in the plasticized media dialogs
And vapid political catch phrases

Make real in our minds the solidity of what lies
Behind the unerring danger of mere words
In the poisonous air of absolute beliefs
Of geopolitical, ethnics and religious boundaries.

Thinks instead of
The blotting effect of sand on the blood
Of the soldier's mortal femoral loss

Draw, courageously, visions of black smoke
From screaming burning flesh in destroyed tanks

Pin onto your heart the common medal describing the last thoughts
Of dying consciousness on the field of battle
And wide eyed children in front of carnage

Do all these things
So that the testosterone driven commentaries
Of the selective memory of veterans,
Of armchair absentees academics
And safely removed three star generals
Be cleansed by the reality
Of this bleeding soldier and the crying mother

For they stand hidden behind
The happy crimson colored flag on some headquarters' map

So that, may a collective feeling of nausea
Be the result of every glorifying representation
Of the killing of one's own
In the family of man

Memorial Day revisited

MARY MAGDALENE

As usual gentleness and evil co-existed…
…and did their best at ignoring each other.

As always on earth… Man had succeeded in juxtaposing the suffering
caused by living among one's own…
…with the imminent salvation of the freedom that death brings.

But it was the presence of the enormous incongruous obscenity of the innate
beauty of natural things…
…facing the ugliness of human actions…
    …that must have disgusted then… like today…
    …the witnessing glance of the Justs and the Moralists…
    …albeit without faith.

The sheep were giving birth in the fields…
and the birds of prey were finding their food hiding under a bush…
…while the last cries of the last condemned were heard between the blows of
the hammer.

As always the mortal life of mortals was following its course among things.

But while the hawk… by imposing death… only nourishes its family…
…Man wanted to resolve the sterile question of the exact nature of the lines
between the earthly and celestial empires.

It is thus in the middle of these grandiose dilemmas…
    …that I fancy seeing this woman…
    …alone in discerning… in the increasingly vague eyes above her…
    …I fancy seeing this crying woman…
    …crying not for a god… nor a symbol…
    …but rather for the man next to whom she had awakened just three
days before.

Mary Magdalene… who knew real anguish.

It is in her that one must find the real… temporal… and individual salvation…

…all of this… in the early signs of a thankful smile…
in spite of the pain… on the precious dry lips of this man.

It is a glance full of tears and earthly love…
    …without tomorrows…
    …the same true glance of the only solidarity between men and women.

Between good and evil... she chooses the familiar.
Between good and bad... she chooses to kiss the solidity of the bloody and dirty ankles of the one who had been in her life.

And in front of posterity... in spite of the knowing intellectuals of things religious...
...in spite of supposedly divine writings and defamatory lies on her future human and womanly value...
...she cries... with no thoughts about herself... for the one who had held her in his carpenter's arms... at night... away from the other disciples.

At the foot of the hard wood of crucifixion... she looks deeply into the gentle and increasingly distant eyes of the man she loves.

A metaphysical thought crosses her mind...
        ...but quickly disappears...
        ...for it is not the coming centuries that is her concern...
        ...but rather how to appease the pain that is wrenching this beautiful body whose supple youth she still can feel.

Her pain and disappointment would be that much bigger... if she knew...
        ...as she shuffles in the blood soaked sand...
        ...if she knew... to what extent posterity would ignore the most important drama of this day:
                ...that is...
                ...the earthly death... and for always...

...of the love of two lovers who are caught in an historical cataclysm that will steal their identities.

Will there have passed by... in each of their minds...
...for a human instant...
...the wish to be far away from this rocky place...
        ...to know... instead...
        ...the anonymous... quiet and daily love... known by others?

From an agnostic passerby... an afternoon in Palestine.

PROTOPLASM

An anti-humanist view

So much mass… so little space.
A deflating globe,
with an inflated view of ourselves.

While we produce and reproduce…
…at the cost and result of reciprocal
…and reciprocating sweat and slime.

Reproductive pieces of us.
And call the result: unique and sublime.

"Why?… why all this?"
An inquisitive sound from mankind
about distant Big Bangs and haphazard molecular existence.
And other inert noises of significance.

One of the many universes whispers in reply:
"I don't owe you an answer…
…go ask your constructed gods."

Overwhelming beauty or stomach churning carnage.
All the same in its eyes.
If not ours.

No Voltairian absentee landlord… here.
And surely, no fatherly interfering and intervention
from old deities in old powdery books.

Complete meaningless void
in which we conveniently find,
with luck on our side,
the personal appeasement in a temporary object of desire.
Apparently and negligently put in our path
to catch and distract momentarily our attention
from eternal mortality.

So, leave it to unsatisfied poets
to make sense of emotional realities.
With pretentious verbal syntax
of delusory importance… like this one.

Amebas and frogs, lion and antelopes
mindlessly copulating and making lunch of each other.
But only man can destroy

the whole carnal, visual, and gratuitous composition.
Calling it meaningful and pregnant with destiny.

I wonder what the skinny sparrows were thinking,
on the leafless summer branches,
in their diminutive non-human brains
...and racing little hearts,
of the intelligence of the soldiers dying of chlorine gas
in the patriotic trenches of Eastern France.

When the last living thing / has died on account of us, / how poetical it would be / if Earth could say, / in a voice floating / perhaps / from the floor / of the Grand Canyon , / "It is done." ' People did not like it here. / 'Requiem.'   By Kurt Vonnegut

With, as background, the scene in the 'Singing Detective' by Dennis Potter, when the voice-over describes his disgust for how life reproduces itself.

BETWEEN SCIENCE AND HUMANISM

Between the two extremes... lies perfection.

Between the two... lies the emotional middle...
...the happy center that keeps things anchored...
        ...in a bi-polar world.

What too often... is lacking in an unjust and inhuman universe...
...that is...
        ...a gentle masculinity...
        ...and a virile femininity.
        ...a maternal view of male induced suffering...
        ...and a paternal kiss to a love starved son.

Between the two extremes... lies perfection.

On both sides of the equation are rock-steady worlds:
Sciences in one... Humanities in the other.

Quiet reflections on evolving theories...
...versus... impressionistic views of the soul.

Two worlds quite happy... living in glorious mutual ignorance.

Until the two collide in the accelerator of life.

Until they are together face to face...
...in an anonymous crowd of people....
...finger food in one hand... the obligatory drink in the other.

Between the efficiency of the metric measuring tool...
...and the descriptive beauty of a poetic essay...

Between the electron microscope in some metallic room...
...and emotion bound words on the scratchy whiteness of a paper...

Between the life saving potions of science...
...and the food of the soul of iambic thought.

Between the two... lies the needed cross-fertilization...
...of what tries to make sense of stellar objects with the elegance of calculus...
...and what tries to capture their flying beauty in a fluid syntax.

...of what tries to bring human warmth and warning to nuclear science...
...and lessons in human weaknesses in biblical texts.

Too often... molecular stability looks with sterile surprise upon emotional flair...
...not realizing that one is the yin of the yang.

That one is alone without the other.
That... between the two... lies perfection

These two worlds... ignoring as best as possible...
...what is on the other side of a paper-thin wall.

Until a chance happening... in a statistically bound universe.
Until a glance... a witty repartee

Chaotic things of the heart...
...talking now... to pulsating electrical impulses of the brain.

Warm glances into another's soul... trying to make sense of bundles of cold photons.

And we witness the colliding of two worlds...
...until now ... deep in reciprocal ignorance of the other...

Falling in love with that which is a mystery in their eyes...
...that which defines us... by what we are not...

We witness now... in the warmth of the unified world...
...the glorious nuptials of the extremes...
    ...which make one...
        ...of what used to be two.

Of a scientist happily married to a humanist

OF SECULAR SAINTS AMONG US

Secular saints are sainted the way societies have often sainted them…
…with bodily violence,
…with personal pain.

Quivering bleeding dying organs versus the linear inert deadly militaristic metal.

The translucent embodiment of Good…
Versus the opaque materiality of Evil.

Secular saints have been sainted by bullets.
Political poison of jealousy and the fire of numerous inquisitions.

They have been made to disappear
Under the anonymous soil of the common graves of the genocides of history.

But the truth of their morality, thoughts,
of their ideas and dreams,
Have never been touched or challenged.

Rather ignored and vilified.
Made off limit to the masses.
Declared somehow dirty of mind and body

Secular saints have been stigmatized and marginalized.
Branded as dangerous and lunatics.

As being members of an avant-garde
Running toward the edge and the destruction
Of the Republic and of good taste.

But the knives, the poison, the flames could not destroy
the molecules of immortal truth within these fragile human sainthoods.

And this truth being…
that we cannot find peace and understanding
in any other place
than the warm tolerant embrace of solidarity
toward this gentle, if at times bothersome, Other among us.

———————————————

John was sainted the way many everyday, practical and authentic saints are
sainted: by being stopped in the fullness of their potential.

Saints are sainted not by society and not by us good middle class mortals.

74

Saints and in particular lay saints... secular saints

Saints of the streets... at the corner of crack cocaine,
Saints of the marches... in crowd control clouds of chemicals.

Saints losing clothing and flesh to insanely trained police dogs.
Saints that know nothing of their own sainthood.

Saints that do not care that they are saints.
Sainthood that wants nothing of its own identity.

Like the Jesus of the Mount of Olives,
they turn away from their sainthood:
having no use for it.

A saint, rather, is sainted by the simple act of its murderer
who certifies, by his inhuman action, to the rest of us,
the special humanity and symbol of this sacrificed person.

The very one who had previously just...
...walked, sung, written, eaten, lived and loved among us.

We think we saint our saints by our public approval.
We think that we anoint them by our plastic television
reverence and appearances

While they often return our respect with disdain or neglect.
Surprisingly... not needing us to get up in the morning

The only goal they have... is the drive to their goals.

And they gather their admission to the sanctum of sainthood
as they are checked at the gates.

The murderers, and the well-meaning judges of good taste and status
stand in sterile mutism as the coffin passes by.
Knowing, in our guilt, that we will have had nothing to do
with the quality of the corpse in the wooden casket.

When their tender flesh was transpierced by the bullet,
we stood by, incredulous,
for we thought that the fervor in their heart,
the purity of their views...
...and their very image among us,
would protect these saints from harm.

It is justly and unjustly just the opposite.
Like canaries in the coal mines… they are the first to stop singing.
Telling the rest of us about the injustice
that is rising in muddy torrents around our ankles.

And we stand, again, incredulously, looking at the TV screen…
…seeing the best among us die…
…sainted by brutality.

"Imagine…" John Lennon

I FANTASIZE BEING SIX FEET UNDER...

I fantasize being six feet under…
Under a ground full of holes.

Full of flesh and bones
Full of sounds of hate and pain.

Oblivious to the above…
I live quietly my hours…
Under ground…
Amidst the muffled roar of war.

I am six feet under…
Under the Ardennes fields

Walking back to the dorm after a World History class

MANKIND AND ITS PLACE

It will be after the last lion will have eaten its last prey...
...it will be after the last volcano will have spumed its last flow...
      ...that Mankind will tentatively be still standing.

In his artificial heart made up of artificial plastic parts...
...an artificial impulse will pass...

...and Man will nevertheless have a human thought upon his imprint on things
and beasts.
      It will be one of sadness and regret...
            ...but it will especially be one of humility and fear.

Mankind will still have a Voltairean glance upon his precarious hold on things...
...the same look that he had on the earthquake of Lisbon...
...with lives sliding off the mud of the indifference of the world.

Having weaved flags and fashioned gods to give continuity where none
existed...
...having crossed oceans and homogenized cultures...
...Mankind will look into the mirror of his deeds and of his history...
...and he will find instead a desperate face looking back...
...one... longing for desperate guidance...
      ...still and always...
            ...ever since scurrying for the first time under a rock during a
            prehistoric thunderstorm.

It is not the sorrow felt for the weaker of the antelope being overtaken by the
hungry lions that we feel sorry for...
...it is the very realization that it... Life... is no different for us.

The gratuity between life and death...
the ambivalence of good and evil... have been such...
...that a veil of good taste and proper decorum will have been spread by us
over their very existence.

And with all of the beauty inside museums and the advances of scientific
knowledge...
...it is the fearful realization... that... in spite of all the separation of artificial
walls between us and the mud of earthly reality...

...we carry no more weight among the rocks and matter that surround us than
the last dropping of the last chicken looking up for a last time at the reddish
flames of an asteroid coming over the horizon.

It is thus with this ugly... dirty truth...
that the solitary agnostic moralist works and battles.

It is in this most honest of open-eyed solidity of things that we can appreciate
fully the ephemeral beauty in our eyes... and only in our human eyes...

...of hills freshly covered with snow...
...of the first smells of Spring...
...of the laughter of children at play...
...of the repulsive beauty of birth...
...of the incredible magic and quasi-religious value of the swooning next to us
in the eternity of a darkened and nuptial room.

The true heroes of this tale will be those who will have glanced without
blinking into the enormous void of things...
...and returned from the precipice to face the rest of their individual lives...
...without whining... without duplicity and especially without eternal laws...
...without guidance... but their own built-in haphazard connections of neurons...

...and who... from this uniform mass of nothingness...
...a form with no front or back... that we call life on earth...

...these heroes... will have fashioned moments of solidarity and a mutual gift
of happiness for the Other...
...and all that... for no other reason than... that they knew that it was all that
there would ever be....
...a gift of meaningless happiness...
...for an infinitesimal moment...
...in a meaningless continuum.

Now... THAT... is courage...
...to look down from the cross... and tell the witnessing audience to love each
other...
...for there is nothing else to look forward to...
...and die with envy... as the kitchen smells of the night suppers reach the
height of the hill.

When the last lion will have eaten its last prey...
...and the last lava flow from the last volcano will have hardened...
...Man will have time to reflect on his status and his actions...

And as useless tears burn the side of his face...
...He will recognize that neither his status nor his actions were of any import or
meaning to the universe... except... except to his own kind...
　　　...and that will be good... and that will be enough.

Reflections on the 2004 Tsunami

OF PRIVILEGED DUCKS AND SOCIETY

A Manifesto for Animals

Just an innocent walk… along an empty beach…
…hat should have remained just a splendid metaphor for my heart…
…along and among expensive and expansive houses.

Glittering blues of sky and water… and late fall sunshine.

Everything to make one forget the unbalanced world…
…and make things right in our mind and under the sun.

And yet…
…call it a European defect… I had to impose my views on this image of
Rockwellian tranquility.

Marvelous fat ducks… of ivory white and shinning black…
…evidently enjoying themselves and taking quick plunges to wet their plumes.
Proudly coming back up into the sun and quacking their approval of things.

And my mind was wandering away from this scene…
…and contrasting it with another.
For… far away from these pampered ducks… off private and quiet sands…
…and safely away from the great unwashed masses…

…my proletariat heart was seeing their cousins in some urban oil infested inlet
just a few miles away…
…white plumage of shades of gray…
…old detritus from street people in their beaks…

And my political mind cannot help but think…
…that these pampered ducks have no more claims…
…to earthly happiness and pleasures…
…than the humanity watching them…
…through filtered windows and aftertastes of dry martinis on their breaths.

THE BIRDS AT SAINTE-MAXIME

Between two Februaries

Today exists between two Februaries.

Near the Mediterranean... life is... of a deep blue...
...and the surrounding impressionistic goodness...
        ...finds its reflection in the gold of a kir pêche.
With a misty glance... full of Labrador...
...we observe at our feet... miraculous flowerbeds.

Near the Mediterranean... where the birds live...
...a Lilliputian war has erupted over crumbs of pizza.

With the wind coming from the maritime pines still sleepy of winter...
...the café tables have started looking for fresh air.
Our thoughts are of this Other Labradorean February...
        ...far away... brutal and deadly.

It is then that we wonder...
        ...if the birds at Sainte-Maxime...
            ...know their own happiness.

SONG OF WAR

Reflections on the war in Viet Nam
"Le plus ça change, le plus c'est le même."

Cry for the Mother... whose child is under the rubble...
Cry for the Mother.

Cry for the Father... when hope has faded... and life is leaving his chest...
Cry for the Father.

Cry for the City... when the cherished trees are burned witnesses to the
shooting in the streets...
Cry for the City.

Cry for the Soldier... whose promise of ribboned glory has turned to reddish
snowy death... or mud incrusted wound...
Cry for the Soldier.

Cry for the Newspaper... whose editor felt duty bound to report subtle lies...
Cry for the Newspaper.

Cry for the Parents... whose vision of a better life for their children has turned
into a fight for survival...
Cry for the Parents.

Cry for the Children...
...and cry for the Sweethearts
...at the train station... at the airport...

See them... see them through red eyes...
...eyeing vague remains.

Cry for them all.

But do not cry for those who... in spite of their training... in spite of their learning...
...have repeated a new sad chapter of the past...
...in the name of the new...
...in the name of the future.

Cry... but do not weep for those whose visions of war...
...are of colored flags and dominoes
...on anonymous maps...
...on cold walls...

Because the crimson on the map
...is the warm blood of Humanity in the fields.

IN RECOGNITION

A painter would offer a cooling breeze over a meadow.
Penitence for the feverish hours.
A sculptor would fashion an appropriately motherly figurine.
The plasticity of clay... given human warmth.

Both efforts would rise from the depth of genuine feelings.

Perfect conversation pieces...
...for some silent waiting room.

A richer man than I... would make concrete his payback...
Strong brick walls for the weak.

Lyricism...
...is the only currency in my pocket...
...with it...
...allow me to distill the essence we all need:
...Recognition.

To the minds who opted for medical research...
...instead of sterile mercantilism,

To the nurses making life-saving decisions as the clock strikes two in the
morning,

For the pain and anguish the staff carries home at shift's end,

For the collective ignorance of this all...
...let us sigh...
...a collective mea culpa.

For their years of application... for week-ends away from their own ones...
...let us not editorialize about the affluence of doctors...
The Olympian wages paid to players of children's game...
...would make obscenity... out of... recognition

This place... is very seldom of joy...
...heard usually... as a crying bundled form!

Its product is more often the reworking...
...of abuse
...neglect...
...decrepitude.
The last cycles of life...

...played on a stage of sweat soaked sheets.
The routine of mortal tragedies...
...and last-second happy endings...
...unrolling amidst the shriek of a heart monitor...
...acting the role of a Greek chorus.

The gentle touch...
...the kind eyes...
...the stern professionalism...

All... in a contradictory mixture of life-saving tubing.
And... escaping life-robbing body fluids.

For all this...
...monetary neglect...
...is too often society's repayment.

Through these doors...
...sooner... or latter...
...we will pass.
Through these doors passes humanity in need.

Let us not... therefore... disdain until the last moment...
...the heroics that await us on the threshold.

We must believe that the sign of civilization...
...is the distance it allows...
...between...
...human needs...
...and its collective conscience.

In lieu of payment for the debt

OF LAW, JUSTICE AND TRUE HEROES

To the Bishop and Jean Valjean

My name is... One... One... Eight... Zero... Seven... Seven... Two... Four...
I owe my past and my future to you.

Just numbers on a name-tag you say... but flesh... and especially blood to me.
O positive it says.
Just numbers you say... but a life and accomplishment offered to society.

In a metallic box... on yesterday's shelf...
...they speak... they whisper... of an anonymous face... with shining officer's
metallic parallel bars on a starched collar...
...a properly efficient and cold secretary in the antechamber...
...all the proper trappings for a cold reception and proper punishment.

"Your son is coming home..."

"...Oh! Thank you... thank you..."

"No... no... you don't understand... He is A.W.O.L..."

"...Oh! Thank you... thank you."

And so... mere mortals have to deal with life altering decisions.
And so... sometimes... some of us... hidden behind unassuming desks...

...are allowed to play the game of the gods.

Crying mothers... dying fathers... disinterested corporals...
...have to face what is in front of them.

Losing a son... and saluting flags... hanging equally and coldly in the balance.

Applying laws... and true humanism... get intertwined in an amoral and infernal
mixture.

And so we have soldiers standing guilty in front of their future and they cry...
...hey cry of both anger and sadness.

They face death from both sides... in their heart and in their bodies.
Nothing will save the father from the years of smoking...
...while military discipline is endangered by emotions...
...its business is that of dedicated bodies.
"He is A.W.O.L... Oh! Thank you... thank you."

And so... the innocence of verbal incompetence for once touches the heart...
The anonymous captain makes a life giving...
...generous...
...grandiose decision...

...he forgives and protects the soldier...
     ... and sends him eventually to a fruitful future.

One... One... Eight... Zero...Seven... Seven... Two... Four...

The future is engaged in this divinely... brotherly gratuitous...
...and... so human... moment.

No need for the images of gods in the pages of Mythology...
...no need for the plastic heroes on the screens of Hollywood...
...no need... even... for the literary image of the silver candelabras on the chimney mantle...

We have... rather this anonymous and real captain...
...in an anonymous and sad barrack...

...filling out... in an existentialist gesture...
...the proper box... on an anonymous form...

...and who then... dutifully went back to his family after his tour of duty...

...unknowingly... having changed the future...

...forever and for the better.

(above) In New York, September 1959, having arrived by boat, Le Flandre, a few hours earlier. My parents would arrive in October but they wanted me to start school on time in the United States. Therefore, I was sent at age thirteen and a half from Marseille to New York by myself with a stop at my cousins' in Paris. While being processed, my suitcase in which I had left my chest x-rays had already been sent on the docks so that my first steps on American soil were at the side of a New York police officer who had to tell my confused family that they would have to wait.

(Jean-Yves Solinga collection)

CHAPTER 5

VOICES

The flip side of love, is to lose that love, "Flower of Paradise." It is the very gentle beauty of Things that make their existence so precarious.

The other side of having, is to let go. Pygmalion in "Galatea Free," lets her go to have her own life.

And even a nonbeliever will have *Voices* reminding him what is, or should be, ultimately the right thing to do.

A little girl senses the guilty soul of an adult in "Does she like flowers?" "Unfiltered Honesty" uses the equivalent of Tourette's syndrome to show that we sometimes tell the real truth while pretending to show humor.

Too often, we find out that the closest thing to possessing something or someone is the feeling of being possessed by it: "Love Hate and other Things."

"And so the World comes to an end" and "Of Sand Dunes and Oases" belong to this world that is so readily accessible through art: fantasy, the unreal. In the first this empty snow covered beach is the setting for an encounter with this "hellishly" dressed gentleman who holds a "bargain" for happiness. It is a poem whose English language genesis is symbolic. The second poem is subtitled "Sunstroke Fantasy." It is a privileged place between sleep and full consciousness where visions are under the guidance of gratuity.

It is mankind's great ability and even greater frustration to conceive of happiness before possessing it: "Down of Anticipation." It is this awareness that makes us get up in the morning. The eventual possibility that, no matter what, we could have our turn to our portion of joy: "For an Eternal Spring."

GALATEA FREE

Love should have sufficed.
But Love, for the rest of us,
does not have the fictitious power of an Aphrodite.
Better believe in Santa Claus instead.

In a grand delirium of lies
that he had for too long been whispering to himself,
he thought he had perceived his own in the reflection of her youth.

Precisely where decrepitude had been hiding:
inside the mosaic of pieces of the present.

Beautiful words… beautiful sentences
made up an ultra-intoxicating light gas.

Making one forget the solid manifestation
of temporal reality:

"When I get married…"
Futuristic image where the object of the preposition
will not be the listener.

Sentence conjugated in the indicative of innocence,
in the optimistic mode of Youth,
and the happy incomprehension of its impact.

The *Ionesco-like* stage turns to black.
The wings are emptied.
He will be progressively alone amidst Things
that learn to ignore him.

This Woman… once so near,
So accessible,
about whom he knew all:

What she would have for lunch…
the shade of her latest scarf.

He is left now… envious… wondering about all things:
Whom she will love,
and what anonymous name she will give
to her child.

FLOWER OF PARADISE

On the warm side of his soul
Had appeared a flower.

And, like all flowers, it was thirsty of warm breezes,
Protective hands and knowing tender caresses.

She offered him, risking her life,
The fragility of her petals and Things of her heart.

Turning his back to the sun,
He was lost in the splendor of her beauty.

He wanted to retain her with his glance
And thus capture her presence in the sunbeams and in Time.

On the sun-bathed side of his soul, existed a flower.
She had found a place there on a day of joyous wind.

She had in her the freshness of things future,
The sap of youth, the humidity of life.

He thought selfishly that she lived through his admiration,
While her roots were looking instead for the solid richness of Things.

It is then that he noticed her stem bending toward the soil.
She was dying in the shadow of his presence.

It was upon moving away from her, one last time,
That he saw her shimmering, up there, all by herself.

And he learned that day, finally and in his heart,
While hearing the whispers of her name on his lips,
The price that is asked of real lovers.

Far away, in Hawaii, lives a garland of flowers

FATHER OF THE BRIDE

Gentle... quiet souls both:
For Her...
Animal whisperer.
Animals of any kind:
Feathered or hairy.
Great protector of butterflies.

For Him,
Enthusiast of the open woods.
Great hunter in his mind.
Yet, proud and kind owner of gold fish pond with invited frog.
But more importantly
Master of summer Italian tomatoes.

Both inspired, if misguided, original sauce makers:
Using aromatic lavender instead of oregano,
With interesting if puzzling results!

Their relationship properly baptized
With the secular wine of Rosé de Provence.
In the warm hedonism of Saint Tropez.

And then, there is the small matter of fatherhood.
Fatherhood which is about protecting and keeping.
Keeping your little girl close and safe.

Things of daily life.
Precious things worth jealously enjoying:
Her grand mother's sauce and pizza top.
Her lifesaving reminders of birthdays and anniversaries.
Her precocious whispered wisdom.

But life, as Jean Valjean learns in Les Misérables,
Life... is about giving.
Not keeping.

So that the future can happen,
It is time for fatherhood to step aside.

For Love... and their lives to begin.
And so it goes...

Inspired by Charles Aznavour: "À ma fille"

DOES SHE LIKE FLOWERS...?

Ten years old, in a gift boutique.
And... she takes charge of a precious piece of my life.
"May I help you?" ...with an assertive voice.
Such a solid presence for such youth.

Man of the world that he is...
Been everywhere.
Man of the world... continental.

Femininity, precocious or otherwise,
They are all familiar objects in his backyard.

Yet... he mumbled...
He mumbled something about flowers.

A series of splendidly innocent,
While very serious inquisitive questions:
As told by the nearby mother:
"Now make sure you ask the costumer why..."

Clarifications and purposes.
Awkward intrusions, it seemed, in his life.
His conscience was whispering to him.

Complete disconnect between
The symbolically pure voice.
The serious purpose of the gift.
Its societal value.
The angel-like face.
And the business-like drive.
He wanted to run out of the store.

Under the charm
He describes the colors .
In material and positioning:
A colorful flower, to hang up.
To attach. To tape up.

A sheet of silk petals.
Sizes and colors... all evenly precious under his glance.

Dazzled, flustered, speechless,
In front of verbal youth

She seems to sense that he sees it.

Out of nowhere…
"Does *she* like flowers?"

How does she know?
What does she know?

His only answer:
"She is a flower of Paradise!"

The little girl wraps the colored silk behind the counter,
With what it seems is a knowing smile.

VISION OF A MOTHER, A SISTER AND A LOVER

Beings, things and places that we have loved.
Beings, things and places that have loved us.

And Time that attempts to erase them.

We try to reconstruct the features of what we have touched,
Of what we always wanted to touch.

Of the object without which, we knew, we could not live.
Or continue living.

Breathing leftovers of culpability, we acknowledge,
in spite of all, our survival in Time.

We mindlessly drink of our cup of coffee,
As though nothing, nor anyone could stop this gesture.

All of a sudden, without a source or sound,
All the past, all the moments come out of the warm emanations in front of us.

Astonished and silenced by all these sensations,
We feel once more the warmth of *her* lips
Enveloping in wavering images this transparent face,
All of this evaporating into tenderness.

All of this in the vapors of a cup of coffee

UNFILTERED HONESTY:

Dialogue within Tourette's syndrome

It is with him that we talk when alone with our conscience.
Or when making believe that we are interested in the color of a new shirt.

He makes us swear that we will not do it again... ever...
"...let her be... you have done enough!"

And then, the immediate object of desire...
...and of visual temptation unfold in front of us.

The past becomes the moment.
We outstretch our hands towards sweets like a little boy.

All the philosophical structures... all the academic lectures...
All the wisdom of encyclopedias rush to our aid.
Sartre shoves Camus who replaces Pascal...
And Rimbaud and Baudelaire are off stage...
...waiting.

Our immortality, our reputation... our freedom of action.
The impossibility of not being free...

And the heavy responsibility of action that commits our future.
All that in the balance.

The family consequences and the societal rules.
All of this clearly and firmly in front of our eyes.

And, Tourette sits quietly face to face.
In his favorite leather chair... the one that we gladly offer to him.

He is at home... he always was.
He had never been chased out...

We could not live without him.
For it is he who gives us hope, real or vaporous, to the last instant.

It is he, who allows us to distinguish the cream colored translucent pearls,
...from the charcoal black of existence.

It is he who lets us close our eyes upon our death...
And who says:
"You did the right thing; in spite of consequences.

You would have regretted it all your life."
And we wake up in a sweat on the moist pillow.
We hear the mechanism of our watch on our forearm...

We can feel a warm moistness at the corner of our eyes.
And we try to fall back to sleep in what is left of our lives.

Tourette's syndrome: He can't help but tell the truth.

DOWN OF ANTICIPATION

Next to the down of Happiness...
...we can feel the smile before seeing it...
...the deep sigh is heard much before its leaving *her* throat.

The near future... where her presence is felt...
Fills itself with a real and carnal ecstasy...
        ...surrounded by her arms and perfume.

We travel through an ambivalence...
...between a calm conscience...
        ...of what is solid and wise... tactile and moralist...
                ...found behind hermetically tight philosophical doors...

...and the other side... the one... where we end up... in spite of ourselves...
one of fantasy and endless semi-consciousness...
        ...so similar to the beginnings of awakening in the warm morning cotton.

It is a region outside of the Gospel... the glance of maternal disapproval... or
family criticism.

It is indeed on the edge of things... that things allow themselves to be perceived.

It is there that one notices the soft waves upon this down...
        ...sensually moving to the imperceptible whispers of pleasure.

Between the sun-kissed flesh and the refreshing shadow...
The down of skin becomes an intermediary.
It allows us to know the most Human of Human experiences...
        ...Anticipation.

Between the flesh tanned by the rays of life... and the Baudelairean hair where

live the hidden dreams...
     ...exists this down of moments to come.

Happy up there... it was as though the few air molecules...
...were maintaining a balance of life...
     ...between a conscience surviving among the four walls of existence...
       ...and the enormity of black and fertile voids of dreams.

In the background of the declination of words...
     ...such as... eternity... and... immortality...
       ...escape the shouts of fear of the unconscious.

An ointment of spirituality invades the smallest dry cracks of the mind.
Solid convictions evaporate in front of contradictory gods...
...between those that promise a tranquil dark rest... and for all time...
...and those... that tempt us by a humid foretaste of seeing *her* again.

She was here...
     ...and she is gone.

And now we must join both sides.
Our arms hurt from keeping them open.
We can no longer touch these two concepts.
Little by little we let our hands down.

We look to the left and to the right.
A nervous trembling above our shoulders announces defeat.
We let go of everything... falling back into the temporal.

Ironically... it is with our arms at our sides that the Crucifixion begins.
We cry... we cry... as the nails of reality enter our flesh.

We hear leftovers of sentences...
     "My presence has made you more spiritual."
And we must choose.

With a spiritual diet... the body will die...
While the soul will be nourished by words...
     ...and we will have the hope of seeing *her* once more.

We make a Pascalean wager... we bet on the mortal enemy of rationality...
...for one day... and forever...
     ...to be able to see... one more time... her presence in front of us.

So we close our eyes... denying our religious beliefs of solid things...
     ...in favor of the vapors of Hope.

Inspired by "La chevelure" by Baudelaire.

AND SO THE WORLD COMES TO AN END

The blankness of the beauty is what surprised him...
...it felt like bundles of electrons in the coldness of cyberspace looking at the
sun of a Monet painting...
    ...and ...nothing ...nothing.

A precious little beach... doing its grayish best in the cold of a gray sky...
...and he closed the blinds.

Beauty... any beauty... hurt his eyes.

He wanted the emptiness of his glance to match the one in his heart.

And then it happened... the ultimate break with his precious past...
...his very body... his very mind... were forcing him to live in verbal reality...
    ...his reflections on this blankness of sadness came to him in the
    other language...
    ...in the common language of *Others*... English.

He was letting go of the intimate cocoon that he had woven...
that they had woven with all their bodily emanations.

And so... as literature tells us... well before the fatalistic event reaches us...
...it is in silence... in whimpering silence... that things stifle themselves.

It is under the half empty sheets that we curl up and swallow hard...
    ...and make noises similar to choking... gasping for air...
       ...not the guttural noises of lubricity...
       ...but those similar to the trashing of imminent death.

Suffocating and sterile half breaths of a half-life... in a half empty present.

And so it came to be... that between snowstorms and remnants of ice on the
sand...
...under the watchful eyes of blue-eyed seagulls...
...looking at an empty beach with an empty soul...
    ...it all came to an end.

And so the world comes to an end... on tear-spotted sheets and droplets of love.
The last efforts are a mixture of grimaces and smiles...
...tears amid ecstasy...
...and the awareness... the physical awareness... that every motion is the last one.

We bend our knee in the crying wet sand...
...we bend our head in the bay wind...

...and we profess our faith...

He whispers:
>...I believe in the immortal value of the imperceptible sighs from her lips.
>...I believe in the eternal value of the gentle pressure of her fingers on my hands.
>...I believe in the absolute truth of accidental words from her.
>...I believe in the inherently religious value of the way her hair twisted on her forehead.
>>...everything else is only pregnant prologue and wanting conclusion...
>>>...and I leave it to the gods.

As he continues his walk on the beach, he is accosted by a beautiful figure in a hellishly flowing silk robe...
...a regal presence on this unstable sand... and no footprints to give credence to his form.
From the vision's mind to his are silently offered pearls of the universe.

In his gloved hands the figure holds visions of eternal happiness...
>"...at a price" he says.

As he reaches to grab these pieces of comfort... he sees the future...
...in this Faustian bargain nothing is for free...
>*...but not every price is beyond the value it represents.*

In this future, he will walk among the damned... but he will carry within him the haughty glance of one with the conviction and memories of their moments of happiness in his heart.

With every molecule of his being he will take his place in front of the wall of eternal damnation with his pick in his hands...
...showing... in his eyes... disdain for the present and immortal pain...
>...knowing that his very glance will have been privileged to see *her*...
>>...in one last and long embrace...
>>>...warmed by the still pulsating hot embers of their love.

KISS AND SILK THREAD

Their kiss was made of the same precious and corporal substance that is silk. Like two beasts intertwined one last time... there appeared... between them... a sticky residue full of tomorrows.

And while their bodies were moving away one from the other... a silk thread started to unwind between them.

All this was happening on some concrete sidewalk chiseled by the frost...
...a boulevard... filled with stern faces... quick glances... stylish dresses...
...and multiple languages... meetings to keep... and letters to mail.

It was only a street... but it might as well have been an ocean.

Their glances were searching for each other on either side of the sidewalk.
It is then that he felt the silk thread pulled to the breaking point.
This substance religiously woven from their lips was unrolling from its cocoon.
The anonymous urban traffic cared nothing about this living organic silk linking them.
The cocoon was losing its yellowish cover as their hearts were emptying themselves of the other's glance.

Coming from their entrails... this animal substance was allowing them to retain a living cellular contact.
Nature had chosen this apparently feeble thread... with no physical pretension... to fight against time... and the moment of separation.

The shining silk of the glance was unwinding and the moment came... when... there was no more...
...no more time... only a last glance.

A last glance... through the buses and the crowd...
...and ...the thread broke.

The thread broke... and... for the first time... it became inorganic and sterile.

This sticky and carnal silk became dead and with no animal future.
And by its death... this substance exemplified a truth full of agnostic... selfish... and hedonistic morality.
That is... that once their bodies are out of reciprocal intimacy...
...once out of what seems to them their reason for being...
...they will return to their inorganic and non-human worth...
...and... only disintegration in the void of things will be left for them.

We learn also... once more... the horrible lesson...

…that to love does not necessarily mean to possess.

For… while looking upon her one last time…
…abandoning her to the dangers of the crowds and noises…
…it came back to his mind that… it is only by unfolding its cocoon that a butterfly can take flight.

All this imagery was burning his heart…
while he once again walked in the opposite direction…
…with …on his feverish lips… the sticky leftovers of silk.

FOR AN ETERNAL SPRING

We take for granted the yearly rites of the renewal of nature
Youth is often jaded by the symbols of Youth.
Indeed, we carelessly glance at the joyful fertilization of pollen-laden bees.
As though it were just their eternal duty.
We expect such rituals from Spring.

The return of the sun's warmth
is assumed to be the product of a cosmological clock.
Thus we see the things of nature
as just following the rhythm toward their rightful new beginnings.
While, unfortunately, for mankind,
we see its inevitable unwinding toward its rest and neglect.

But once in while, in our garden,
a bush, a stalk, a fragile flowering tree,
overlooked and unloved,
is found by that wandering bee,
is touched by a friendly gardener's hand.
Catches the kiss of a warm evening breeze.
And Youth, and Passion
and the sublime flow of life returns.
And our eyes witness what is meant by: loving life again.

For souls who find love again

LOVE, HATE AND OTHER THINGS

Reflections on Liaisons dangereuses

Feeling disdain... then... for her as a prey,
Pain of satisfaction in my body as she laid...
                                        easy claim.
Out of my needs,
As she answered any of mine:
My eyes finding endless imperfections
            in my new-found possession.

Pain of surprised frustration:
She turned down my invitation!

Wounded spirit flying barely off the ground...

Sweet jealousy: building her to celestial dimensions!
Widening distance between us... filled with evil imagination.

Becoming... in her absence... no less than the Ideal,
She must be completely mine to be real!
As I stand with unbelieving eyes...

Detecting... now... a certain disdain in *her* smile.

THE INSTANT OF THE LAST GLANCE

The Artist, Inspiration and Time

His words were forming a translucent lace.
A clever netting where the spaces and knottings
Were magically linked.
Only his art could give birth to such filigree.

His words came out, sliding, still warm,
Wrapped with the glue of life.
They came out effortlessly, with barely a contraction,
Almost painlessly.

He covered his solitary moments
With this grammatical balm, and all was well.

He scrubbed with force this lyrical substance
Into the wound caused by the voids of his soul
To cure him of shivers caused
By the absence of conviction.

He gladly talked about his literary fantasies:
Santa Claus and grandiose Faustian oaths,

>   Of Proustian Essences and lyrical reconstructions.
>   Of obscure Parisian cemeteries.

And although he felt at ease and proud in the soft dawn of his words,
Protected from reality by a selfish artistic intoxication,
Manipulating antitheses and digging into the historic lexicon.

He needed instead the daily, earthly, human solidity
Of the tactile presence of an embrace behind a closed door,
A crusty warm baguette,
The exotic essences of a couscous.

It is still with these words that he tries today
To recreate these visions,
With words that he tries to rebuild the moments.

It is in the remnants of where she is not, where they are not,
That a smell of death reminds him of anti-poetry, of silence.

The stink of putrefied flesh
That is the mark of lack of inspiration.

Perverted, diabolical, blaspheming fantasies
Call for the destruction of the written work.
He now knows, deep inside, multiple emotions
Of jealousy, hatred… a feeling of sterility.

And yet, that is what the artist faces with a white canvas.
All that is left for the ink stained fingers scrapping musical notes.

The artist makes use, far from the source of his inspiration,
Of the deadly and suffocating heat. Of the silent space
In front of which he manipulates words on a screen,
Touching a plastic keyboard.

The artist uses words, only words like a pubescent boy
Finding sterile and personal pleasure in the corners of his mind while thinking
of her.

In this private and hidden activity,
His seminal lyrical essences
Evaporate without fertilizing anything.

His thoughts run the risk of being only stains
On the rich thick paper made alas of dead cellulose.

He now knows that it is henceforth
Only with words that he can caress.

His fleeting thoughts turn to Rimbaud.
Was he correct to stop his art?

Putting an end to the toxicity of dark ideas
Talking about an unreachable desire.

Happiness it seems, defines itself by its absence.

We are now at the instant of that last glance.
This ultimate moment of the last salvation of the artist.

Hoping to see his object of desire offering
Him the keys to enter the eternity of Things

That moment where the contact of our left ear
Is with that precious chest,
Where is found all that counts on earth.

Recognizing a similarity in this glance

With that of our mother during our childhood fevers,
We will know at that instant that all will be well
As we give, from our lungs, back to the universe,
What rightly belongs to the universe.

At that instant Things will shrink to a tunnel vision
Where images of our mother, our sister and our lover
Will melt into a warm glance.

A flashback takes the artist, automatically and corporally
To a scene of his youth.
In the dark of a dark bedroom where he opens his eyes
And begins to pray.

Only to later notice that he has been silent.

Surprised he begins again.
To find that his very body keeps him from believing in this deception.

He refuses to talk to God the Father,
While his own, his father... reality, the mortal,
Is dying at the rhythm of the cancerous creaking of the mattress springs.

He tries to pray, nothing.
It's the end.

No longer will he feel the tranquility of knowing that things
Follow themselves in an orchestrated cadence.
Nevermore.

He will have to live in a world where the dangerous can swallow you gratuitously...
just like that... by chance.
In a creaky, infernal cacophony.

So he decides that all he can hope for
Is a loving human glance upon his dying body.

In a world with no absolutes and moments of intellectual arrogance,
In a world with no ex machina references,
He believes for the first time since youth.

He recites his creed:

"I believe that Things are the way they are because Things wanted them so.
In spite of the created taboos, I have always loved life
And don't remember not loving it."

AGAINST AN ETHIC OF THE MACHINE

Between the flesh and plastic

Electronic sentiments, alone in the room.
Alone at the table, alone in front of a coffee cup.
Alone in front of the machine.

Electronic sentiments, our molecular warmth filtered,
Purified by a circuit. No breath. No sighs.
Just transistors.

Elementary particles: constructed by others, for general applications,
Without particular reasons. Product of anonymous technology.
Ready to say anything to anyone

Pieces of intelligent marriages of exotic metals
And of unbreakable plastics.

Dumb electric circuitry.
Numeric language, written in foggy syntax.
Worthy of the great priests of pagan temples.

The whole contained in its modern plasticized box
Attached by its electrical umbilical cord: its vital essence.

Compatible with all conceivable human feelings:
Without for that matter feeling any of them

Electronic sentiments. Our seminal residues absorbed.
Orphaned and neglected.
Along the copper covered wires that know nothing of life and tears.
These sentiments not recognized, nor admitted.

This newfound human technological sensitivity knows nothing.
And their users gently brush against it with trembling fingers
During sleepless and solitary nights,
As they attempt to reconstruct,
Based on dead impulses of blind photons,
The tears of ex-lovers on earth.

Like pimps, interested only in the farcical aspects of loving,
They bring together the miserable and make them believe in the virtual.

Human thought, rich and tortured, full of anguish and laughter.
All deconstructed.

Reduced to trigonometric electric curves on an oscillating current with no interest.

Deconstruction of man and woman.
Human warmth that one tries to rebuild through the coldness of electrons
Saying intimate things through technological distances.
Using pieces of silicon to express the needs of the flesh.

Feelings, souvenirs, sighs.
All sent through the grinder of the entrails of a computer.

They all became sterile by their intimate closeness with the dull and dead vibrations of the machine.

To be eventually reconstructed, expanded,
Like some coffee crystals in water. More chemical that thirst quenching.

And then the moment comes when you realize,
In a moment of anguish, which stifles pain,
You realize that the face you are looking for
Cannot be reconstructed.

And all the smart programs, all of man's impressive technologies,
Cannot render the plasticity
Of the precious skin around her fingers.

Cannot give an instant of intimacy to the heart.

And thus, we are left with empty arms.

Our fingers alone on the black and cold keyboard of the machine.

While this adored face, that we were reconstructing on a base of electrons,

Is lost in the body of the machine, that looks back impassibly.

OF SAND DUNES AND OASES

Sunstroke fantasy

He was parched by thirst; but not passion.
He was enveloped by heat; but not animal.

He had walked through droughts
Under disinterested suns.

He could sense his vital energy
Used only for instinctive survival.
Dissipating into the arid sands of neglect.

His solitary sweats knew only sterile endings,
With no reciprocal echoes, nor promising tomorrows.

His skin wilted by years
Was searching only for frigid comfort
In dark puritanical corners
With no nuances or surprises

Darkness where one knows
Beforehand all the hiding places.

The few appearing oases offered no astonishment to his eyes.
The tepid water of their wells smelled of stagnation.
A stale mortal wind was trying, mechanically, with no conviction,
To sway the tops of dusty date trees.

Things were aging under a sun bored by the empty rituals.

That is when, from a sky blackened by heat,
Close to the fatal moment when one gives in to the inevitable,
To sweet and expected death,
From the gods that he despised so…

…It is then that this magic oasis appeared.

Inexhaustible water.
A liquid, that the gods themselves envied,
Burst at his feet.

Not just a prosaic, chemical water;
But a molecular one: syrupy and sugary.
Complex and drinkable.

A liquid for elixirs and feasts.
Those that will be remembered in the peace of old age.

He saw again, trembling happiness
That he could touch with his lips.

Like a drunken bumblebee full of pollen,
He let himself be covered with the solemn religious powder
That jealously surrounds the tabernacle of sensuality.

The same powder reserved for the initiated
Of the eternal act,
That lets the chosen ones enter the trembling warmth of the universe.

He was lost in the black triangle
Where wisdom gives way to passion,
Abnegation to fervor,
As they come out from their veils of reserve.

The same drive that attacks sleepless
Herds in the field under the starry nights of Spring.

Mankind comes by, but once in while,
Upon these magic oases,
That make you forget and push back the
Stillness and dryness of the desert.

In them we find the balm that takes temporarily away the pain
Of the wounds of an absurd world,
Having seen ourselves orphaned meaninglessly.

On the outskirts of the oasis
The hyenas call to each other from atop the dunes,
While inside the black triangle,
We fall asleep in the essences of the perfume of fertility.

(above) Roman ruins (third century BC) of Volubilis near Meknès, Morocco. Notice the storks during the winter months.
(Jean-Yves Solinga collection)

CHAPTER 6

BETWEEN THE FRIEND
AND THE LOVER

With art we can make one of what is too often separate entities that ignore each other. The coldness of scientific research and the humanity of the researcher, the emergency room of a hospital and the natural sensuality of a nurse, the masculinity and femininity in all of us, the inexplicable oneness of lovers. So it is in this chapter of poems called *Between the Friend and the Lover.*

The overlapping of masculinity and femininity in most of us: "Café Femme" and "To die with Disco and Ambivalence."

The reversal of roles from the dominant to the subservient in the game of love: "He looked down." The lack of logic of feelings, of a sister soul, that would make one of what in reality is two: "Two Beings in the Same Flesh."

On the anniversary of September 11, 2001 there is the bitter sweet awareness that life continues in the same place where we all had heard the news. And yet, there is the hopeful signs that things will be all right. There is still the sound of lyricism nearby.

The characters of "Meursault and Faust" are used to define the ultimate duality of man. Meursault is the consummate protagonist of the Absurd universe. A man who mechanically lives his life with the awareness of the meaninglessness consequences of his decision making. And then we have Faust, who does find reasons to live and meaning to his life and will do anything for a second chance.

To reconcile what seems to repel each other. To see sensuality in the last breaths of cardiac death: "Between the Nurse and the Machine." Laboratory attendants falling in love in and around the sterility of medical research: "Between Science and Love." The childhood images of innocence reflected by the fields where this young woman preparing her wedding is saying her goodbyes: "The Fields of Innocence."

BETWEEN THE NURSE AND THE MACHINE

Fragility of existence
Nagging suspicion of its loss
With no pretext or apology.

Fullness of life replete with Beaujolais and Roquefort.
Un-American Memorial Day
Made of andouilles and chicken livers.

Then looking up at a shaking white ceiling
Of screaming ambulance.
Oxygen leaving his lungs

And vision of a lump of flesh
On a lump of earth
The whole becoming the proverbial dust.

Anger, anger, unfathomable anger
For loving life and losing it!
In the emergency room feelings of regrets

For neglect of the body
As the last scenes are played out
On functional hospital sheets.

In a place of sometimes last-second happy endings
Unrolling amid shrieks of heart monitors
As Greek chorus actors

In a place of late recognition on his part
For the life-saving efforts of anonymous others
A place of payback and perspective.

Where a painter would offer a landscape of
Cooling breezes over peaceful meadows.
Where a sculptor would fashion an appropriately Motherly figurine:

The plasticity of clay given human warmth
Would provide perfect conversation pieces
For a silent and worried waiting room.

A richer man, than I am, would make concrete his debt:
An addition of strong brick walls for the weak.
Lyricism is the only currency in my pocket and so, with it,
I will offer a distillate of my feelings.
This place is into the reworking of abuse,
neglect and decrepitude

playing themselves on the last cycles of life.

He feels guilt for his jaded attitude in front of the heroics bestowed on him:
as someone is gently and quickly shaving the chest hair
to attach the heart monitors.

Surrounded by the stern professionalism,
the kind eyes and gentle touch of others.
Surrounded by a contradictory mixture
of life-saving tubing and escaping life-robbing body fluids,

He looks in amazement over to his right arm.
His academic concept of the predominance
of his humanism over matter is challenged and shattered.
All his intellectual ability and values
come down to the efficacy of the plastic tubes running into his body.
For the first time, since his leaving the womb
with his umbilical cord still intact.
He is completely connected... helplessly connected to the physical universe.

There are times we should remember
not because they are pleasant or unpleasant
but simply because of what they hopefully teach us.

Surviving a heart attack helps prioritizing
between getting angry at a speeding ticket on a previous Memorial Day
and just hearing the heat of the sun at noon time on the back porch while
sipping a pastis.

He hated seeing Time evaporating in front of his eyes
as he gazed into those of others around him in this emergency room.
The rhythm was cadenced by the regular chest pains.
It seemed that his very humanity
was being drained by the whiteness of the room.

He could feel tears on his cheeks.
They seem to verbalize in their language
the symbol of the nectar that he would leave behind
as a token of his love of life
to those that would have negligently stepped
into the liquid on the side of his bed
had he died.

It came to be that between his left and right arms existed all the extremes
that life can sometimes put at our disposal.
On one side, all the attributes that are necessary
to go on about living;
and the other, all that is good about living.

One purely corporal and functional;
the other carnal and spiritual.

For on one side he had an infernal machine
automatically and blindly taking his blood pressure
on the other side the gentle blond and sensual presence of a nurse
that brought, by her very presence close to him, chocked sounds of regrets in
his throat.

And so it, between the machine,
doing its 'automatic' best... and the negligently-placed thigh during a pulse-check,
existed the entire and terrible equation of man and nothingness
beyond the philosophical musing of academics.

At moments like these, there is however not enough energy or time
for a well thought out existentialist pensum.

Between the machine and the nurse
he was thankful that the happenstance of things had put this object of desire,
at this critical time, so close to him.

He was even more thankful that this was happening with his face in the shadows
of glaring unforgiving lights
for fear of her seeing in his glance the last vestige of passion in the middle of
physical decrepitude.

Between the nurse and the mount of dying flesh lacking in oxygen are the
dissipated remnants of years of carelessness and excess.
Between this silky white presence
and those of the machines with streaks of lines on their faces
palpitates the chest that refuses the inevitability of death.

The pale, quiet and humane face of this woman contradicts the coldness
of the crazed numbers of the blue plastic boxes that reveal the defeat of the body.

Between the electric blue of her eyes and the plastic blue of the machines he felt
guilty of the worst
of humankind weaknesses':
that of not having loved life enough.

His lips let go a great sigh at the moment
when the very *materiality* of his body intruded into the spirituality of the love of life.
The sensuality of this nubile woman rendered him deaf to the screeching
mechanical alarms
acting as that of this dramatic Chorus prophesying the death of flesh.

And on this hospital bed was the scenario
where the plot of life and death was played amid the acrid smell of cold sweat.

IDYLL OF GUINEVERE AND LANCELOT IN NEW ENGLAND

Cats are cats… and love is love, you say.
And the two should not mix.

Tell that to Gwen and Lance.
Symbolic lovers of the kingdom…
…animal that is.

Of dubious ancestry. Murky morality.
And rumored incestuous leanings.

All stilled into platonic friendship
By divine Vet intervention.

Not perfect mascots for impressionable college youth.
Yet lovable in the warmth of the sun.
Touchingly very human in their ways.

Source of serenity, solace and perspective before exams.
Some tuna cans and a scratch on the belly as easy pay.

And we can all enjoy seeing again,
Pieces of the eternal glory of Arthurian legend,
In the court… and in the yard of… Larrabee,
Where medieval lore and love live again.

To 'Gwen' and 'Lance;' two stray cats.

BETWEEN SCIENCE AND LOVE

Somewhere in the antiseptic environment of medical research,
In spite of the air filters and scrubbing equipment,

Sneaking around the safeguards of infectious diseases,
Smiling at apocalyptic viral spread,
Unafraid of worldwide microbial threats,

The wild-eyed bug of human love
Took hold in the midst of sterility.

The fragile glance of friendship,
Of ultimate and tender affection, could not be killed,
Vacuumed or autoclaved.

Chance meetings under romantic neon lights.
Half-started sandwiches,
And half-finished conversations.

Haphazard brushing between a cold chair
And a metallic research bench.

Crumpled warm personal notes
In top pocket of white lab coat.

"Five o'clock, at the front door:
I have to feed the cats."

This world of science and cold logic
Would eventually be infected
And happily fertilized by what it is all about:

A commitment to what it means to be alive
And what life is meant to be...

Love... very human.

CAFÉ FEMME

A Sexual Manifesto

"Ah!... So it's a *café femme* that you want?"
Heard from the virile waitress's voice.

Surrounded by women in this restaurant run by women.
Was I accepted in their solidarity?
"Yes, a café femme." Shyly.

Having let on about my dual background,
Through some words in English at the table.

"Well then, a *café femme* for the gentleman."
Were not the women in this coffee house having any?
I didn't dare ask.

The *café femme* states certain truths.
It appears under a serious and black form.
It defines itself by what it is not... what it is no longer.
By what it refuses to be any more.
Submissive or passive.
But rather, uniformly strong.

It still exists under the look of a coffee house waitress.

"Ah!... So it's a *café femme* that you want?"

You are put back in your place by the candid remark.
Prejudices and stereotypes go by in your mind.
They are recognizable in the aroma of the coffee.
In its sugary and raspy texture on your tongue.

But all is said when my masculinity is dissolved when faced with this dark glance.
This boyish hairstyle.
From a woman and a coffee house that put things back in their places,
There where they should be... where they should always have been.

This revealing cup of coffee.
The need to understand this statement.
The coming, one day, in a glorious and innocent ambivalence...
...when the difference in taste will be purely personal,
And not associated with our sex.

TO DIE WITH DISCO

I want to die with disco invading the room.
Vibrating the death defying tubes in my nostrils.
Giving organic pulse to the inorganic liquids.

Words of immediacy and instant gratification,
While life holds only minutes for me.

Images of tortuous gyrations on parquet floors,
While eternal immobility is taking over me.

No concept of time as the night is young,
While having heard in a whisper that it would be my last.

Spinning globes and caged dancers,
Nubile bodies and eternal youth.
Visions of the plasticity of flesh,
Amid the dryness on my lips.

Boum-boum... boum-boum,
May the primordial vibrations replace my dying heartbeats.

Boum-boum... boum... boum,
May the waves of sound give to the sterile white sheets,
The appearance of hidden lubricity.

Complete decadence and Faustian pledges.
Destruction of the soul and burning bridges.
Nothing to lose for nothing to gain.
Still though... hoping Saint Peter is a swinger.

As I close my eyes... I swear I can discern a sway,
Under the silky whites of the head nurse.

Taking a certain, unexplainable, enigmatic,
Smirk to my grave.

To the beat of : "That's the way... I like it..."

AMBIVALENCE

It's in the music.
It's not in the "going-to-the-office body."
But it brings it out.

From the deep.
The reptilian deep.
No rules and no prying eyes.

The senses. The sensuality. The fantasy.
Out of body experience,
Without the impending death, trauma,
Loneliness and single sterile white light.

Just joy and transport to the other side,
Under multicolored filters.
And the immediate company of a glorious
Self-pollinating humanity.

It's not the singer's fault. It's his voice.
His masculine lows and plaintively sensitive highs.

It's not his fault... he's just a conduit.
A go-between.
A shape in a mirror.
An androgynous inkblot.

The last note is played.
Time to go back to separation
And solid segregation of right and wrong.

But what a walk!
What a peek!
What possibilities!
What a walk on that side!

What does it say about me?
My swaying hips,
Still tapping feet
And papers to correct?

Let's dance... David Bowie

A STONE IN THE DESERT

Reflections on Marguerite Duras' "The Lover"

And so, at the end of strength and life,
Void of yesterdays and tomorrows,

Blinded by whiteness of nothingness,
He falls to the sand of stellar dust.

In front of his eyes... a stone,
Full of the death of petrified hopes

Solid with the dryness of not-taken-alternatives,
Emanating the foul smell of fear and regret.

And he gazes upon it...
Its solidity contains his immobilized existence.

And so, he closes his eyes in fatalistic abandonment,
When he sees a drop of blood breaking out between the inorganic crystals.

A sticky whitish liquid oozes out of the sterile mineral
Smells of lavender fields and floral explosions sneak out of the stone.

After all these years... after all this distance...
After all the silence and attempts at blanking out the past.

The last vision... the last smells... the last tactile sensation before his death...
Of trembling embraces and pregnant gazes

All will be in this Paradise Lost... in the humble form of this magic stone,
In the desert of his life.

BETWEEN THE ARTIST AND INSPIRATION

At the temporal limit of Love

At the temporal limit of Love we enter in a rarified world of the impossible... and inhuman choice.

A choice reserved for the gods that inhabit the space between the lines of literature.

It is the place chosen by the playwright with a drab and dead personal life... ...who presents to us between stage right and left... remembrances of breathless moments of fervor.

It is the subject of crippled and half-blind painters who remember... like yesterday... the shivering warmth of pink feminine flesh under the impressionistic shade of poplars trees.

It is the central theme of sickly, drug addicted... abandoned writers... ...now alone in their seventh Parisian floor alcove... ...describing for us still and always the most beautiful poetic moments of life... ...the perfume she wore... the way her eyes closed upon a kiss.

It is thus from the pieces of the unreal... left in the corners of his mind... that the artist reconstructs his translucent vision of happiness on earth.

Like the reflection of love in the loving glance of the being that we love...
>   ...to know that upon our awakening she will still be asleep next to us.
>   ...that we will know together the too often neglected joy of evening shopping at six o'clock at the corner grocery store.

And then we wake up... our fingers still on the keys of the machine... ...we wake up in the mud of reality... ...at the limit of temporal love... ...there... where we ask of man... in all his weakness... and especially in all his cowardice...
>   ...to choose.

To choose... on one side of life... between the stability of the daily routine... the invading decrepitude... the solidity of the noise of people passing in the street...
>   ...and... on the other side... this refreshing but vaporous cloud...
>   ...of the impossible...
>   ...of the untouchable...
>   ...of her glance...
>   ...of THIS glance.

It is then that reality wins…
…that happiness becomes a fantasy… something to which we have no or no longer a right.

And we begin to write or paint again things that do not or no longer exist…
…if not in the heart of the artist…
…and on the canvas of a museum in front of which the tourist passes…
    …with envy…
        …holding his breath…
…wanting in turn to have known the source for this inspiration… now eternal.

Inspired by the movie "Young girl with pearl earring."

HE LOOKED DOWN

He looked down.
Virginal pink… rushing to his cheeks.
His eyes wouldn't meet hers.

Painful irony
Debauched body… ashamed of its effects.

Lifetime of precedents…
Leaving him with ever-renewed virtues.

Oh! Sweet Venus… what eyes!

No shame meets his.

Irresistible call of Nature…
Pity him… he sees Paradise.
The Lord Himself… he would forsake.

To Hell… he'd send his bones…
For a drop of her sweet sweat.

His thoughts were just frustrating souvenirs…
Offering themselves…
As hopeful tempting tomorrows.

TWO BEINGS IN THE SAME FLESH

From the passion of Blaise Pascal to the hedonism of Albert Camus

It is upon looking into the jealous and voyeuristic mirror...
　　　...where the precious image reflects...
　　　　　...that we see ourselves at the gate of immortality.
This earthy vision... gives a divine measure to our human status.

This ephemeral moment... in the totality of things...
...is the only... the true one... that could rival with the eternal one of our absent
and disinterested gods.

An immortality... in this case... outside of the walls built with blows of Gothic
stones... that surround the divinities invented by and for our fears.

The same one that demands a belief in the tender illusions found in the images
of museums...
...the same one that offers us the stupefied and stupefying glance on things full
of images and the imagined...
...the same one that lets us sleep at night... believing in a tomorrow full of solid
and correct things.

While lovers, orphans that they are, fight with the only weapons that their
bodies... and only their bodies represent and offer to them.

In an absurd and flamboyant majesty...
　　　...full of sweat and sighs...
　　　　　...the ephemeral quality of their sinuous frolics is emboldened
　　　　　in denying the very existence of this blind and deaf universe.

And all of this... through the joy they witness... for a few instants... in each
other's glance.

The world of things... cold and sterile since the first explosion of matter...
...the world of things... showing off the scientific beauty of its galactic spirals...
...the world of things... overwhelmingly proud of its elementary solidity and
chemical eternity...

...face to face with our spiritual fragility and molecular mortality...
　　　　　...can only witness... in a silence...
　　　　　　　...full of rage and envy...
...the miracle of the intertwining of these two lovers.

Because, in spite of all its strength, the universe cannot make a single thing out of two.

While... it is upon seeing the reflection of two bodies in the mirror...
...that they recognize that there were two beings...
　　　...where... they had sensed only one.

121

THIRSTY MIRAGES

To know that one is loved and to see oneself travel through ecstasy...
...to taste from it the excessively natural and very material beads of sweat.

And then... to hold happiness between your humid fingertips and to feel life escaping from them.

To know the solidity of joy... and to feel now in your heart only its illusory transparency.

That is when you realize that the magic of the gods lies in their using the disorienting landscape of the deserts...
...full of mirage like thirst and false paradise.

We try to run on the powdery sand of the dunes and we run out of breath in front of the object of desire that disappears on the other side of the crest.

Even less substantial than the vapors of yesterday's flower...
...there remains only from her the debris of a presence that we now question: a paper towel... the coffee in a cup... a wrinkled pillow.

It is then that... from all that is ugly and sterile... comes a somber certitude.

From nights with no sleep and peace... comes forth the awareness of the inevitable:
It is that which makes us already miss the present.
It is that which makes us afraid of the moment of separation well before separation.
It is that which shows her facing our tomb.
It is that which shows her reading our words without our being able to absorb her precious glance.

From the pain that crushes our soul comes a shameful cry:
...one that calls for an end to this temporal agony.

It is then that a huge knot of disgusted infamy keeps us from speaking...
...we understand how the first Christians... face to face with the worst of pains... could not disavow the things of their hearts...
...anymore than we can... face to face with this very earthy image of happiness...
...full of pearls of immediate joy...
...of hope with no tomorrows...
...and of agnostic certitude...

      ...and all this in the earthly silt.

Love and the inevitable

THE FIELDS OF INNOCENCE

Somewhere between the field of innocence and adulthood... lies life.
Somewhere between the light green of the blades of grass...
...and the blue green of the glance... of the eyes of youth...
    ...lie images of a faithful and protective yellow dog.

Somewhere in our heart we can still find...
...this unpretentious little path to a clearing...
...this clearing exists in our visions of a younger universe...
...still empty of the hurt and loneliness from Others...

"Moon River... wider than a mile..."

It is a time and a place full of potential and dreams...
...of timid awareness of a timid... but flowering femininity...
A time of spiritual ease amidst the common... yet eternal beauty of things of the earth.

Just a field... to those privileged enough to be allowed along...
...but more precious than gold to her...
    ...for it lives in the precious whiteness of innocence of the past.

"Moon River... wider than a mile..."

Gone is the Madonna-like hair... on a doll-like frame...
A young girl... doing young things...
    ...in the protocol of life... and the unwelcome pressure of the rites of passage.

"Moon River... wider than a mile..."

On the other side... we find the harsh solidity of the demands of reality and society...

And so... between the field of innocence... and the age of remembrance...
...we find that we have left the best behind...
    ...somewhere in the blades of grass...
        ...and the disappearing footsteps in the early frost.

All that remain... of the field... of the shy frogs... of the grayish rock next to the brook...
...are the crying strings of violins... and an almost feminine tenor voice...
    ...on a scratchy vinyl record.

"Moon River... wider than a mile..."

A young woman on a stroll through the fields of her parents' house before leaving towards her life.

123

LEATHER AND FLESH

The jackets seemed to talk to each other...
...their leather squealed against the other.

These animal skins were replacing with their groans...
...the throaty... but human noises... of two intertwined beings.

These skins... long dead... shaven... and unnatural...
...were regaining life through the vaporous passion of the bodies they covered.

The leather was answering with almost animated warmth...
...the rite... and animal rhythm surrounding it.

The wrinkling of things... in an ever repeated and eternal act...
...was the whisper... of universally understood... non-verbal noises.

Both leather jackets had regained the youth of fields opened to the spring sun...
...they were reliving moments full of tomorrows...
...they were yet again engorged with blood.

And while all this was taking place in a frigid moment...
    ...full of darkness
        ...and hidden from view...

...for a few moments... this leather would know again the happiness of the everlasting...
    ...tactile...
    ...wavering...
    ...silky...

    ...smooth and quivering... love...

    ...of flesh against flesh.

MEURSAULT OR FAUST?

In the uniformly black background of an agnostic universe...
...a philosophical and linear peace reigned.

The sleepy hallways of the morning gave way to those empty of the afternoon.
And the shiny light at the end of each of them was only an illusion...
...without particular value... without ultimate joy... without redemption...
and especially... without goal.

Life was a routine... that led to no more than a middle class or philosophical
happiness...
...satisfied with itself... and the moment.

Things and beings regularly brushed against each other without much knowing
how or why.
The brutal solidity of the first and the carnal fragility of the latter ignored each
other...
...each camp believing that it could live independently in a perfectly chaotic
and gratuitous universe.

The crossroads of life would confront us from time to time... without thought...
at our feet.

And... in this universe reigned a similarity full of anguish...
...between having a cup of coffee...
        ...stopping at the toilets...
            ...or the survival of a sick child.

Things and beings were prisoners of a universal and eternal ambivalence...
...and all was well.

All was well... among things... and beings...
...and amidst the somber awareness that...
...the future was no more valuable than the past.

_____

Until the day... the minute... the second... when the apparently solid edifice
collapsed entirely in powdery fragility.

We start to ask:
        ...if ambivalence reigned...
        ...if divine or material a priori did not exist...

...why then... *her*... and not another?
...why then... *this glance*... and not another?

What is the origin of this spontaneous and solar presence, which now fills our sky with multiple suns?

Which other laws of things and man are now transgressed...
...and... *can be transgressed?*

From the depth of our being... feelings boil...
...that cause fear by their openness.

We feel possessed by an irresistible urge towards... *freedom... fantasy...* and *dream.*

At night... under the pillow... for fear of being heard by the gods and man... we ask ourselves...

  ...what if it were only this *glance* that mattered... *and nothing else?*

Unthinkable thoughts emerge... limitless possibilities assail us... and invade everything.
A rare feeling of gratuity reigns... such that Meursault himself would cry like a little boy...

————————————————

And so... we begin to dash through all spaces and all times.
A mind altering tempest... worthy of all the illicit formulas of all the alchemists... opens up.

Our soul... yet recently unreligious... cannot now... turn away from the call of this new religion...

  ...blind... blinded... and blinding... love.

It is then that we repeat with fervor unknown to our heart...
...the Creed, which will guide our existence henceforth:

"She has had several lives... but one soul...
...in another life... she lived for me...
...I know it... I feel it...
  ...she was my sister...
   ...my lover... she was I...
    ...I see myself in *her* and her glance is mine."

To live in other lives... where the temporal limit to embrace... would only be that of passion...
...where laws would have as limits... limitless amoral and selfish needs.

To live in a world where the beautiful Lucifer would find ease outside of the city of God...

...having decided long ago... not to attack the divine fortifications...

...but rather to settle in the surrounding forest...

...with things and people whom he loved and loved him.

A world without claims and without black fears emanating from the dark closets of life...

 ...where Evil would just be another way to live.

The true... and original innocence of Paradise:

   Adam and Eve... still not knowing that they are naked.

All the laws... and all the taboos... do not or no longer exist.

And in spite of all the virulent plagues of the past... and the destructive asteroids of the future...

 ...all these other instances could only have led...
 ...to this *kiss*.

  ...and nothing else.

The certainty of the absolute of the Absurd facing the illogical nature of Love. Or the inevitability in Buddhism meets Camus

To the music of Your Kiss *by Hall and Oats.*

BETWEEN INSPIRATION AND NOTHINGNESS

The gods with their lightning bolts...
...set fires to the dead and dry twigs...
...in the silent and puritan savannas.

A pagan fire... in our entrails...
        ...which forces one to create.

Oh!... but to taste fully... the poisonous and biblical fruits of hedonism.

These are the same divinities that left us behind...
...to keep alive the flame of inspiration and prevent it from dying from the winds
of forgetfulness.

They are the ones who gave us a taste for the sensuality of sight...
        ...and the fear of losing it.
They are the ones who gave us the craving to tell...
        ...and the fear of having nothing more to say.
They are the ones who put the object of desire in our arms...
        ...and its powdery disintegration on our fingers tips.

To feel this precious object dissolve in front of our eyes.
The need to write faster... to avoid losing the moment...
...surrounded by the deadly fear of rote writing.

And so... we touch with our fingers... things from her.
Quasi-sensual fondling which attempts at reconstructing the past.

The gods gave us the taste for the eternal...
...and the evaporation of moments of inspiration.

They are the ones who made us taste in our heart... the bitter remains of the
awareness...
        ...that love alone...
        ...love in its complex purity...
        ...does not give to its lovers...
        ...the right to love... and this... forever...

These same blasé gods gave us the taste of parted lips...
...and the horrible sensation of knowing that embrace is not timeless.
That the sweat soaked emanations of the present...
...will face the blanched skeletons which will have lost the quivering of life.

It is then that we decide not to venture any further in this desert of tomorrow.
We let ourselves fall on the sand that is already burning our feet.

We let ourselves go in the darkness amidst the whiteness of the crystalline minerals.

To let oneself die... facing the sun...
...to hear... no... to listen...
        ...to the rubbing of the sand next to our ears which sink in the dune.

We hear the cries of a bird of prey...
...this is the last breath of a universe calling us back to life...
...and which now leaves us ambivalent.

Just before our death... a flash of precious images appears...
...these used to give meaning to our life.

And so we die... the way one falls asleep...
...disdainful of a world where...
        ...love alone...
        ...love in its complex simplicity...
        ...does not give to its lovers...
        ...the right to love... and this... forever.

———————————————

And then... just before we enter eternal happiness...
        ...we awaken to the much too common daily noises...
                ...everyday silt acting as a Greek chorus for a background...

We wake up in a universe guided by rules and morality.

And so we set again to write...
        ...all this in a world where...
                ...even love cannot stop time.

Reality versus Art

BETWEEN TWO SEPTEMBERS:

Between the platonic and the carnal

Between two autumns exist two beings.
And between the two, only their glance remains.
The look into the eyes is the last link when words are prohibited.

Between the carnal and reason exists thirst.
The thirst quenched in the humid remnants inside Yesterday's eyes.

Between two Septembers lived two souls.
They cross fertilized each other in spite of the drought brought on by mortal
And cataclysmic events.

In the midst of a cruelty with no redemption,
In the midst of Things changed for all and forever,
They looked upon each other… and saw only the other.

Whispers of nothings and phrases of endearment,
In their loving and loved language,
From which they had constructed a protective cocoon.

And in this desert from human love, political and global,
They had found each other, peacefully surrounded
By the most fragile of flowers.

Like in these sterile deserts, where
A rare rain, calls back to life the prodigal daughters
To their nuptial duties full of pollen.

They drank life in each other's presence,
The way these gentle eyed animals, touch tenderly
The lukewarm waters with their lips
In the center of the killings of the Savannah.

Between two Septembers, remains only this table,
Spot of their first mutual glance,
Across from which *she* remains untouchable,
     Protected by the *masculine* frankness of her glance
     Which nevertheless allowed him to possess it and possess her.

Between the platonic and the carnal
Lies a classical tale.
Made of very human but special beings.

A Tristan facing his Isolt, to whom are left only
Quick and knowing glances
That allow him to recognize in her the adored and scented fruit.

Exiled from earthly Paradise yesterday,
They realize that time affects them now.
Death is starting to stalk around their passion.

Waiting for an eventual rendez-vous
In some surrealist cemetery
Under the warm Southern sun.

This cemetery is at the intersection of the realities of life
Where are found inevitable death, duty,
And the whitish clock on the wall.

The formers will have all conspired.
And all will be lost.
They will not live happily ever after.

And just when all seemed frigid in its eternal frigidity,
He heard his words coming from her mouth.
She had made hers his words.

His ideas were living through her body, her lungs. Her lips!
Between the platonic and the carnal
Lives a piece of happiness.

His words in her voice were the fruit of a glorious sensuality
A very human, agnostic, personal and hedonistic epiphany

She had, with her lips and his words,
Joined what had always been separated in time:

The platonic from the carnal,
The smoldering heart from the warm visceral.

To love after the hatred of September, 2001

(above) One of the entrance gates to the Holy City of Fez in Morocco.
(Jean-Yves Solinga collection)

CHAPTER 7

DREAMS AND REALITIES

In this chapter I have called *Dreams and Realities* there is the universe where we dare acquire: no! demand our piece of happiness. There are no physical restrictions in this new dimension: "To Wake up next to the Sun, the Moon and the Stars."

These lines look at both sides of the consequences and decision making. We explore that border where morality and abandonment to natural instincts fight and overwhelm each other. The most prosaic of places, a lunch table, can be the take off point of an encounter with the gods of destiny: "Black Butterfly." The everyday surroundings of office work can lead to the opportunity for escape and hedonism: "The Lacework of Happiness." A peek on "The Other Side of the Wall" where we discover that we had the solution close at hand all this time.

What if we had what the gods take for granted? Instant gratification inside "The Candy Store of the god." What would happen if there were no consequences or taboos in the candy store? The happiness of the innocence of a little boy?

What if you were in middle of happiness and love, and you could "feel" the loving glance like a silk cloth being gently pulled on your face: "Seeing oneself being loved?"

What happens when you find out that these taboos and realities exist. That these circumstances are becoming old, "Iced Grass and Lost Youth," where we lose everything but the passion. What happens when you transfer a dusty medieval tale of the impossible, forbidden love of Tristan and Isolt to modern times with the accompanying accoutrements of guilt and unstoppable lust flashing on the car windshield in "Proustian Essence?"

RESERVE AND PASSION

A certain reserve in her demeanor.
A restraint of the Soul.
Not wanting to see it splintered.

As though she knew, as though she feared.
As though she were conscious
Of the danger of letting herself go.

As though a protecting voice had been saying,
Well before the Kiss,
That it would be All or Nothing.

An extraordinary lubricity to safeguard:
For her self-esteem, for her dignity.
So much in danger, was she, of not wanting to control herself.

While looking into her eyes: a few inches away,
While holding her in his arms,
While feeling her against his chest,
While seeing her confidence in him...
...for the first time.
And then letting herself go in front of his stupefied glance.

At such an instant full of the warmth
Found in the whispers from the shadows of the curtains.
At that instant, he learned of the hidden intensity of her desires.

And the fragility symbolized by the nervous and blossoming beauty
Of the wide opened gentle wings of a butterfly... under the Sun.

THE GIRL IN THE SILK DRESS

Shrouded hopes under multicolored silken cloth,
This flesh, halfway between the statuesque
And the sinuously palpable.

Pose full of reserved sensuality,
In which he chooses to read the embers of their intimate secrets
Behind the gentle complexity of the gaze.

Object of desire that had satisfied everything to the limits of everything,
The envy in his eyes losing itself in the limitlessness of hers.

Tightly held knees that tempt the eyes
And sculpt the hidden creases of flesh
Folded in the carnal feast of remembrance.

Surrounded by the beautiful Maghrebin murals,
A translucent porcelain seated amid the turquoise mosaic.
A pearl, color of the very milk of fertility.

Exotic voyeurism of the surroundings
Explodes in his soul with no guilt.
Pardoned by the natural beauty of this vision
Which has found in this setting of protected privileged shivers,
The symbol of her gift of true quasi-virginal voluptuousness.

My vision of a harem. Following Delacroix's: "Women of Algiers in their living quarters"
and the book of Honoré de Balzac's "The Girl with the Golden Eyes."

TO WAKE UP NEXT TO THE SUN, THE MOON AND THE STARS

Gently closing his eyes made of sleep,
Next to a human made of fervor.
Only a sheet of Egyptian cotton threads between them.
To go to bed with a woman,
And waking up with pieces of mosaic of the Universe next to him.
Touching preciously this cotton that hints of her flesh through white translucence.

To go to sleep with a human being, and wake up with…
The Sun, the Moon and the Stars.

Moments that put Heaven on Earth,
And God again in a dead heart.
Bringing back the magic of a Christmas morning
Under a Christmas tree.
To make the ephemeral eternal and the mundane spectacular.

To go to bed with a woman and wake up amid the Sun, the Moon and the Stars,
Spinning around her in her presence.

To hold the secret to the secrets of Happiness,
In the reflection of the deep black of the pupil
In the deep color of the iris.
To find in them the secret of solar explosions
And eternal spinning.
Darkness of space in the darkest of eyes,
Put him back into the smallness of his place in the immensity of Things,
Witnessing all of this from his submissive place next to her.

To go to bed with a woman.
Wake up with pieces of the Universe next to him,
That make dead Pharaohs and Roman Generals envy life again.

Pieces of sleep and dreams
reconstruct themselves over the waves of her curves.

With unremarkable ingredients, with feet of clay,
He builds a mortal construct of dreams with unrestricted boundaries and perfect
expansion.

All of this as he tries to touch with human fingertips,
The pieces of the Sun,
The milkiness of the Moon,
And the blinking of the Stars.

Inspired by Jose-Maria de Heredia's (1842-1905) "Anthony and Cleopatra"

MULTIPLE REALITIES

Before us, the straight line of our life.
> We turn around.

What appeared, at first, unavoidable, immovable and fatalistic,
Is not the case any longer, and never was.

In the dark background full of things and people of our past
We can discern the backwash of the abandoned side of the road.
Soft and idyllic prairies.
Black and fertile forests, full of alchemy.
They are the overlooked possibilities of yesterday splits in the road.

Moments and feelings full of promises
That exist only in their aborted futures.

And it is then that we become aware in spite of the solidity of the cup of coffee
between our fingers:
> Of the elementary fragility of our past and present
> Of what we believe we know
> And of the consciousness of multiple destinies.

On the straight line of the road we pass by a face
The way one crosses a car
This image disappears little by little in the rear view mirror of culpability

---

Just before disappearing forever,
We see once more her shape on the film of the windshield of remembrance.
The same face, the same smile, the same body
> The same eyes.

We thought them, after a wisely based decision, well behind us.
And suddenly, here again is all this past.
A few inches from us, pulsating, warm and carnal
Like the first time.

Proustian Essences, 'revisited'

EVERYTHING IN A LOST EMBRACE

*"Mes mains dessinent dans le soir
la forme d'un espoir
qui ressemble à ton corps."*

*"My fingers draw in the dark
the shape of Happiness
that has the curves of your body."*   Gilbert Bécaud

Could it be that everything is in this?
Every meaning and every moment?

Could it be that in spite of believing in nothing,
That a glance would encompass all the other things?

Pieces of nothing, of dull routine: all of it.
But a glance, warm and solid,
As the revered wood in this university café booth:
Etched with the disappearing initials of lovers

Unexpected fingers conveniently finding his.
Caffeine for exam mornings.

Her head popping in the doorway:
"Good luck!"

Signs of quivering future happy moments,
As her lower lip breaks into a smile.

At the shimmering flatness of campus pond,
Her left thigh as warm as the side of the cup.
Their conversation as dynamic as their minds.

Remember, my friend?

What do you do, now, with your detached philosophers?
Your yellowing terminal diploma?
They had filled seriously the voids of the serious soul;
But not the parts that count.

To be resigned to die in the peace of emptiness one day.
And crave for a Faustian bargain the next?

Ready to give everything for an extension
For that ultimate academic existentialist paper.

A little more of something.
Anything.

A chance to stir a second cup of coffee with someone's next to him.
Wayward nail clippings.
Anything.
Youth, maybe?

Fingering her absence.
Her moisture,
Upon finding her handwriting on a piece of paper,

Feeling the void so much more
By comparing it to the emptiness of the moment,
To the incredible,
To the glorious,
To the molecular sweetness and wetness,
To what used to be…
      …her presence.

He starts to feel,
In the gentle headiness of semi-consciousness,
The fluttering of a butterfly on his forehead.

It softly lands on the side of his left eyelid
And extends its tenderly virile proboscis.

It gently drinks the last humid patches from a body
Dedicated to the impossible.

PROUSTIAN ESSENCE

Between Tristan and Isolt

Unexpected moment. Transported into a future
Where Proust, himself, would recognize so well
The fervor, the passion.

The ephemeral quality of the eternal
Reconstructed by a gesture in time.

Far from a religiously and gently sipped herbal infusion
In the quiet of a maternal kitchen,

Fingers clenched on a stirring wheel.
Closely watching the moving shadows
That he believed were coming to life behind every bush in his headlights…

…He unknowingly brushed his right index by his nostrils.

It was as though his body wanted to remind him…
In spite, without, outside of himself… of her perfume… her smell.

He had forgotten that his right hand had held her.
But his fingers lived in memory.

They were bringing her back in front of him.
Coming out of, and released from, the pastoral blackness
Of the isolated fields. On this hypnotic road.

She came to him. A living thing. Straight from his memory.
From his flesh that he was pressing
Into this inorganic and now useless stirring wheel.

Those fingers that had skimmed her body
Rendered partially naked by the cut of the dress.

He wanted to recreate a woman,
Existing in the astonishment of the moment.

A woman existing in the surprise of passion.
A woman existing only in time past.
Time and woman, both vaporous.
Without substance and without return.

From the ordinary value of this gesture
Came out a rich and privileged alchemy.

An alchemy made precious by the randomness of formulas,
Themselves lost in the whimsical mixtures concocted in the middle of the night.

An alchemy rendered that much more irresistible
That, in it, reigned the irrational.
With no shame. No religion. No culpability.

A world, made dangerous by its love
Of the "moment worship" with no tomorrow.

He knew this perfume well.
There should not have been any surprise.
And yet, here he was.

While driving, he brought these fingers to his nostrils.
Somewhat of an animal gesture. A primitive reaction.
As though to determine *its* fertile worth.

He should have been ashamed; but there was no time.

A whole spectrum of sensations opened up.
The smallest details of the evening came out of his entrails.

All of them still warm, steamy with the very passion that had given them birth.
They then spread themselves on the coldness of the windshield.

He was almost in pain.

The magical sorcery of her perfume had this time
Given life to remembrances free in time and space.

Aromatic and solar essences of floral petals…
Glorious synesthesia of the warmth of the flesh transforming itself into a bouquet.

This mixture had acquired a priceless value.
Such as the one of medieval potions that lead both to ruin and happiness…

What emanations! What delight! What nectar!

This perfume, could on its own, bring back
What nothing else could have:

Her very presence.

If Baudelaire had known Proust

ON THE OTHER SIDE

Reality... the other side of happiness.
Time, plays for its favorites... on the side of reality.

Meters out these precious moments,
As though we were not entitled to any of them.

And so we live our lives,
Getting up in darkness.

To drive in twilight to work.
Our heads still full of sleep.

We generate with enough caffeine,
Enough energy to make enough decisions.

During the day we warrant our paycheck.
We are so much in reality... that...
We cannot conceive of another dimension... another *presence*.

Like these explanations of multi-dimensional worlds,
We fantasize about what is on the other side of the wall.

In the middle of a meaningless meeting,
We attempt to fly above the metallic table in front of us.
We escape out through the glass of the window without breaking it.

In these multi-dimensional worlds,
About which we can only dream,
We are not bound by the mud of reality.

A being raised in a two-dimensional world...
...could only fantasize about a third dimension.

He would not know height...
        ...everything would be left or right,
        ...never up or down!

And so, we are convinced that we are wasting our time,
Looking any place else for anything, or anyone else.
This is the way it is... always was... always will be.
Until... until...
        ...we find out that she exists for us... and always has...
        ...on the other side.

OF MAN, BEASTS AND NOTHINGNESS

And so here we are...
...in the center of things... and rightly so...
...we whisper with a righteous rictus on our lips.
Machination and regurgitation of previous beliefs.

All this force-feeding... imposed and self-imposed...
...of images of our own importance...
...and narcissistic longing on the beauty of our deeds and reflections.

And everything is all right. Everything in its place.
That is... far below our human plane.
Until... until the day of a prosaic event...
...taking the garbage out...
...on the coldest of coldest nights of the Labrador.
The snow of sounds of broken glass pellets...
...lungs of sharp darts of cold... and nostrils of icicles.
And nowhere the sound of life...

For, where are the animals of summer... getting ready for sleep or night prowl?
Why do I feel guilty that they are going to stay out tonight?
How do you explain the patently unfair... unjust...
Obscene presence of Life if it is thus?

Why do we put it above the tranquil stillness of stupefied rocks?
What would have been the essential... the existential difference...
...if eons ago...
...no particular adaptation...
...no proper balance of gases...
...no amazing property of water expanding as it freezes...
...and no magically positioning of the lunar orbit to form tides...

...what if... no Life had evolved?

No Monet you say... and Mozart would have been quiet...
...but no painful joints would have plagued one...
...and mortal fatigue the other...
...and no one... no one... would ever know...
...no one here... or there... or anywhere... to KNOW.

Eternal quiet and eternal non-happiness.

And no Roman Legionnaire to die with his intestines and life leaving his body...
...in the middle of the Germanic mud of the Rhine.
And no man or woman would have to answer unanswerable questions from

the Inquisitor...
...before red hot metal would pierce the body.
And no soldier would have died in a darkened jail cell in darkened Africa...
...over some unexplainable tribal or historical boundary.

None of that... but quiet and mortal stillness.

And birds would not have to shiver and die...
...under the leftover of autumn leaves in the stillness of winter.
And a raccoon would not have to scamper in the frozen underbrush...
...to find a meal... and kill life... that would in turn... define his life or his death
and that of his family.

And, thus... all would be right under a non-molecular sky...
...looking down on a non-molecular world...
...that would never have known the descent of amino acid.

And all would be well... not knowing anything else.

There would be freedom from the awareness... of awareness.
And injustice, pain and anguish would weigh the same...
...as love and happiness...
...in a time and space...
...void of both.

Albert Camus felt that the awareness of Life and Death was a sort of joke played on mankind by the gods

ONCE UPON A TIME, THERE WAS A BUTTERFLY...

There are times in our lives,
During unexpected and privileged moments,
On the other side of a door,
On the other side of a conversation,
On the other side of a sip of coffee,
There are visions, so fragile in Time,
That we are afraid to look upon them directly.

Like these pagan rites where it is forbidden to look upon their gods:
For fear of becoming blind.
For fear of knowing too much.
For fear of not being worthy.

There was, once upon a time, a red and black butterfly
That he was watching from the corner of his eye.
It seemed to him that his very glance could have wrinkled its wings:
So ephemeral was its beauty and transparence.
As though, the very weight of his admiration could have crushed it.

On the other side of his closed eyelids exists a butterfly.
It landed upon the lace that makes the fullness and emptiness of the fabric of
our days.

It is on the filigree of the cloth of remembrance that it lives now,
Protected from the destructive rain that threatens things temporal.

Like an idealized dream, full of Platonic colors,
He must today close his eyes in order to see it.

Lost in the grotto of remembrance,
He can only distinguish in it, upon the smoky walls,
The chaste shadows of his carnal joys.

The pure and gentle fiction of the fairy tales,
That the index finger of a little boy
Carefully follows in the large glossy pages,
Becomes, with the years, ironically more real and believable,
Than the lesson of wisdom from our mother.
And especially more solid and interesting than the inevitable stellar void that
awaits us.

These reading passages that produced so much marvel in our youth,
The images that allowed us to fall asleep with a smile on our heart,
Cause us now, to cry in front of their splendid possibilities of innocence.

Instead of accepting the mashing of teeth of our daily lives,
Instead of closing the book full of the unreal and of tales:
In order to face the Serious and Adult of our lives straight on,
We become aware, one solitary day, in front of one solitary cup of coffee,
That we want, instead, to enter, more than ever,
In this world from which we have been chased.

We want to live in this universe of images and symbolic material
That was so close to earthly paradise.
The one of youth which believes, still and always, in the Happy Ending.

The latter, completely gratuitous.
Asking only for a deep belief in these pictures of a hero and heroine,
Drawn by beautiful color pencils with wide open eyes full of surprise.

But, we dare, instead, open our eyes and let reality invade our world.
We must be a "big boy."
We try to convince ourselves that this vision of a butterfly was nothing more
than the dust of boredom.

That what matters after all is what we will have for tonight's supper,
If the garbage will be taken out,
Or if the bathroom faucet will be fixed.
Solid things, that please us by their metallic coldness.

Things that anchor us in the mud:
In the temporal moistness.

We hear wise things from the adored lips:

"You must no longer live in this fantasy…
It will hurt you… it will cause you harm…
To you and to me."

It is then that we close our eyes again.

On the side of the sleep of Youth, we see the shape of happiness.
We live, happy, in a world whose entrance price is the level of fervor and
availability.

A smile comes to our lips… she is here!

And then a noise from the surroundings brings us back to the other side of sleep.
It is the heavy and inorganic sound of reality,
Which falls loudly on the pitiless tiles of life.

We go down the blackened staircase of the present,
Holding onto the familiar handrail that we know so well.
We peer through the large living room door,
And tears come to our eyes.

We have just recognized the features of our father in the man under the
Christmas tree.

And so we go back to bed:
Having learned all that we need to know about life.

That is, that too often it is better not to have seen the Promised Land.
For, like Moses, we will, thereafter, only die of thirst in front of our object of desire.

Although, the fervor of the little boy which continues to live in us,
Will have us believe, until our death,
That Santa Claus, Paradise and this Black Butterfly,
Will come back to this side of our eyelids.

There are times that visions in our lives leave us with our eyes wide open,
Speechless and alone, with only butterfly dust on our fingers
And questioning the reality of what we have just witnessed.

THE LACEWORK OF HAPPINESS

Between the smooth skin and the silky cloth is seen the lacework of happiness.
Between the innocent and careless pose and the small of the back...
...is seen the forbidden object.
Between the double meaning said by chance...
...and the virile feminine laughter...
...is heard a lust... doubly loving and loved.
Between the skin and the lace exist the needs of the present.

And it is in this very present that we begin to hear sounds that chill.
We begin to put nuptial moments in their travel cases.
Looking out of the porthole... we see the land that brings us back to reality...
        ...it lives in time and space.

It is then that an uncontrollable Faustian sigh comes from our lips...
        ...we do not have lordship over what we see...
        ...we are jealous of not having... no longer having...
        ... *Time*...
... *Time*... the only thing that the universe itself cannot ignore:
        ... *Time... and its End.*

Condemned to an intellectual voyeurism.
Seeing the humidity of the object of desire... and to die of thirst.

Seeing the doubly loved and doubly touched object...
...and to open the door of departure... with a frozen smile and a heart full of
regrets.

Tasting once more and always the nectar of flowing things...
...and losing one's breath:
not because we die...
not because the molecules stop vibrating...
not because the body does not crave any longer...

But because Time wants it thus...
        ...and knowing that the future will never be any better than now.

Taking quick steps toward tomorrow...
...and seeing in it only waterless dust...
        ...of the very lust that we hold in our arms.

Knowing that the horrible clock leads to the cooling of things and the flesh.
And knowing that... in spite of the young passion of an old thirst...
        ...it will lead back to a platonic tranquility...
... to the still chaste... and trembling... first embrace.

Ah!... how can we forget this injustice that...
...only these moral souls of the stage and literature...
...in spite of their immorality...
...are allowed to know the great loves of history.

Envious... as we are... of prosaic moments of prosaic people.
Wanting to know the routine of middle class...
　　　...such as looking at each other with...
　　　...triumphant eyes full of sleep...
　　　...on a fertile morning...
　　　　　...intertwined in the eternity of momentary sheets.

With the flow of days drowning in Time...
...seeing just about everywhere... symbols that recall youth...
　　　...a fold in the cloth of slacks... that hint at a secret curved shape.

Between the chair and the office desk is revealed a natural and nubile vision...
...much like these primordial women in exotic documentaries...
...bent at their tasks...
　　　...sitting on their heels...
　　　...touching unconsciously their own beauty...
　　　...preparing the daily meal.

Between the hips and the small of the back exists the voyeurism of privileged silky body hair.

Dédoublement of the being and the vision...
Voyeurism of escapism that suddenly returns us to the reality of the moment:
　　　...leaning against a classroom board...
　　　...or the inanimate screen of a computer...
　　　...reading with no particular conviction the official notice of the day.
All these empty things... of a life filled with old echoes.

It is then that the mind rushes toward the impossible...
...between the skin and the lace... exist ideas...
...without wisdom... without restraints...
　　　...out of breath and stifling.

In this much feared glacial future... we will be left then...
...with only splendid memories...
...and the firm truth... that to have been loved...
...allows us to face death...
...without even deigning to bother looking at it face to face.

THE CANDY STORE OF THE GODS

Upon entering in the Candy Store... they notice... on their left...
...their favorite sweet.
Unknown to them... it had been waiting for a long time... on its glass shelf.

They had almost forgotten its raspy sweet-sour taste...
...which left the remains of a very earthly happiness on their lips.

Rushing in... they stop...
...on their right...
...a beautiful chocolate display...
...the same one they had tasted on their first communion.

Since their first conscious moments of good and evil...
...since their first venture into the hunger of things that surround them.
In its reddish cocoa wrapping hides its intoxicating elixir...
...the same one that offers man a virile vision of his immortality.

A little further... amidst the rich wood paneling... one is aware of a smell...
...no... more like a vapor... a smell from the soil...
...which reminds us of a church festival under the summer sun of youth...
...the same summer in which a little girl in a flower dress is still dancing...
...the same smell of the call of earthly things...
...different and hidden... to the eyes of a little boy.

In the middle of this splendid temptation of the senses and of the body...
...one learns that the first calls of the sensuality of youth...
...were only a foretaste of those of the future.

A Faustian whispering is heard through the Candy Store door.

They had gone by this place a long time ago.
They protected their glance with a middle-class... puritanical... and wise gesture
of the hand.

They used to live... like other mortals... with the certitude that certain happy
hours are reserved for the divinities...
...who... in turn... lounge sensually amidst rules established for them.

They then learn... that they have come by chance in this Candy Store reserved
for the gods.

Two beings... much human... hunger in their bellies... are now... in the Holy
of happiness...

...without much inkling how... but knowing very well why...
...that is... to get to know *ultimate ecstasy*.

Surrounded by all these objects of desire...
...one loses all lucidity...
...they let themselves be possessed by animal need... slave to the moment worship.

Fingers touch everything that they crave.
Lips nibble everything that they touch.

It is in this moment that one hopes to die...
...satiated among all this wealth of sweetness.
And one dies...
...with one last earthly image...
...the last melting crystals of our first childhood candy...

...in front of our eyes... as a little child.

Having all you ever wanted

SEEING ONESELF BEING LOVED

He could see himself loved... He could see himself being loved.

A look... a sort of pout: seen on classical masks.
A state between ecstasy and pain...
        ...a grimace full of love...

That was trying to understand what she was feeling.
That seemed to ask what her body wanted of her.

That was searching in his features...
        ...Themselves full of questioning...
Answers to her own questions.

With little head movements... from left to right...
And yet with a fixed look,
She was taking possession of him with her stare.

He felt intimidated... as though he were reading his own virility in her eyes.
A surprising and masculine aggressiveness was answering his initial confusion.
Her love had conquered all the obstacles that society had imposed on her.
A state of grace was combining... in the alchemy of senses... with a carnal state.

Under this questioning and surprising look,
He felt a nakedness of the soul...
The same that we know only for a few privileged times in our lives.
That of... *the first time*...

The same that makes us put our hands in front our eyes...
...out of fear of what one sees...
...out of fear of what one is going to see!
The same one that makes us modestly protect our sexual organs with our hands...
In the mannerism of these Renaissance paintings showing us an Eve coming
from Paradise...
        ...knowing the very carnal truth of things.

This knowing look... was putting him face to face with a new truth...
The one of his rebirth into a hedonism of long ago... and wisely quieted...
        ...and now...
                ...awakened.

It was an enormous and anguishing middle class fear...
        ...of what we feel surge forward from our bodies again... and always...
        ...of what we want to do again for the first time.

It was a primary glance on her part...

    ...a primordial glance...

    ...a reptilian glance... going back to what we really are in the elementary blackness of creation...

    ...when our culture...

    ...our social graces...

    ...our mannerisms...

    ...the protecting overlay that shields us from our everyday responsibilities...

...leave us... naked... face to face with a world that calls us...

...to answer the great call of Nature.

Lying down... intertwined...

But... unfortunately dressed in garments that covered their bodies as well as their susceptible consciences,

Unable to taste the ultimate hearty goods...

Those that allow people to enter...

    ...quietly and with no hurry... into Things...

Those that know nothing of time...

    ...like a beautiful hourglass with a feminine shape...

    ...but one with no sand...

        ...with all the physical attributes of time...

    ...but without its arbitrary imposition!

They thought of themselves outside of Time!!!

That's what it must be... to be Santa Claus... to feel yourself part of eternity: although the time of departure is near...

To believe that the warm embrace between two beings will not know...

...or be aware of...

...the laws of the stars...

...and that the latter will die only with ours.

That eight o'clock at night will never come.

That... duty will disappear in the fog of the pressing demands of love.

That... by the very fervor of the moment... the moment will last forever.

That Santa Claus in his splendid innocence...

Will bring... casually... with no after thought...

Cakes of desire without limit.

Lips that will know nothing of the wrinkles of time.

And then... turning around he finds himself alone.

With only leftovers of these few moments found in the crushed creases of a pillow.

BLACK BUTTERFLY

Black butterfly...
At the crossroads of the laughter of the gods...
...lived two beings who said... very human... little nothings to each other.

As for the gods... who know nothing of the precious value of time to mortals...
...they were bored by these two parallel lives.

Sleepy and aging everyday existence dominated one...
...and a young nubile future... the other.

"Why not introduce a Faustian fever in one," they wondered?
"Why not introduce into them... godly measures:
That are... superhuman... inhuman?"

These two beings will know the love of the gods... untouchable love.
A love that will burn their bodies from an invisible source.

We will show them the promised flesh... and like a confused and delirious
Moses in front of His vision... they will remain frustrated.
They will turn their envious glance
And their empty heart away from what they love.

From an enormous cloud rains down a musical cadence.
Lyrics... from the language, which overwhelms him...
The language that was present at his rites of passage...

"I want to kiss you all over... and over again."

Love, which comes to you without looking for it...
The love of words said haphazardly in a ... chanceful encounter...

"...Are you the French girl?"

And then... they slide into things,
Which have vanished long ago into the pockets of time past.

Black Butterfly... that one sees land on the other side of a cold cafeteria table
Full of frigid and tired anguish:
...teaching schedules... medical bills to pay... upcoming medical appointments
to forestall decrepitude...

And... amidst this daily debris:
This Black Butterfly... lands into his life.

"I want to kiss you all over... and over again."

She... she now carries the weight of all that is beautiful and valued...
...of all that is durable...
...of all that counts on earth.

While this minuscule and fragile animal represents...
...now and for always...
...what they cannot...
...and what they apparently must not possess in life...
...Faustian happiness on earth.
...the happiness of one who wakes up too late to worldly attractions...
...the happiness of one who... like a slow-witted Gulliver finding himself tied
 by ropes of culpability...
...while all around him...
...on this nude and savage beach...
...the cry to life resonates in his ears.

"I want to kiss you all over... and over again."

His irreligious heart knows now what abstinence demands from them.
From a surprised agnostic view...
He understands better now those who live in God and for God.

He knows... better than all these men and women
Who live amidst things that are defined by what is decent and good...

...He knows what it is... to prohibit the body from having the body it craves.

He knows what it is to see... to touch... to fill his nostrils
With what puts him the closest to eternal happiness... and to tell her...
...May God take care of you...

May God take care of you? ...he does not want her in the arms of a god...
He wants her back from these gods who have everything...
...and like Sisyphus... He will dare confront them.

"I want to kiss you all over... and over again."

...which is still and always ringing in his ears...
...which is still vibrating with the sounds of their first meeting...

"Are you the French girl?"

He felt the fluttering of her wings well before feeling her trembling in his arms.

With the taste of a horrible coffee on his lips...
He was trying to observe her slim fingers,
Which seemed too precious to be holding a common slice of bread.

It is when she was looking away that he could see the blood red lipstick,
Which had begun to burn his soul… well before her looking up.

This black butterfly seemed to him full of sensual fragility.
And while the life of a butterfly lasts but hours…
He did not realize that their time had already been counted.

He realizes today… that it is this animal… ephemeral and fragile
Like its powdery beauty…
…it is she… who would survive him…
…and she… who will offer to those… passing his tomb…
…the blushing images of passion, which she had witnessed…

This same passion, which will burn her black wings,
Still moistened by their love.

…this beautiful animal, full of nervous silence,
Will land on the puddles of salty corporal nectar…
…she will die batting her wings which…
…with natural grace and without anguish…
…will declare… gently…
…that they have loved each other.

"I want to kiss you all over… and over again."

Their lives together will remain forever
At the silky and innocent stage of a cocoon…
Yellow shape full of possibilities and surprise.

She… will always be in the image of things
Hiding under a verbal double meaning:

The sensuality of physical touch…
…foretold by just a glance…

The fullness of sensual intimacy…
…foreseen by a still chaste and yet strong embrace.

How often had he mechanically discussed the dilemma of Corneille!
Chimène and Rodrigue had become… in his heart… but just artificial
characters.

Exaggerated caricatures… persons who did not know how to grab happiness
with both fists…
…and savor it… savor it…

Who were these beings that did not know the taste of happiness?
Why would the artificial restrains of their conscience be a guide to them…
…mere mortals?

It is then that...
...he heard himself say... to his astonishment...
...to defend himself...
...to defend her...
...to defend them...

"What makes me worthy of you...
...IS... what makes me turn away from your love."

The world of literature had once more invaded his reality.

"I want to kiss you all over... and over again..."

...which now disappears in the ambient noise of his conscience.

Classic theatre and forbidden love: A contemporary view of the Cornelian dilemma.

ICED GRASS AND LOST YOUTH

Passionate youth...
Single-minded minutes.

Refused the warmth of the bed:
Turning instead to the iced grass...
...of a winter's field.

Overlooking the cold probes of stones.
Hands... finding warmth... more than lust.

Time playing on the side of Temperature.

Passionate youth...
Disregarding the unpromising future:
Playing with the Now...

Purposeless relationship...
...but instead...

The birth of lust.

Not a purpose...
...but a rite of life.

We keep the passion...
...but we lose the youth.

IN SEARCH OF ABSOLUTES IN THE TEMPLE OF HOPE AND REMEMBRANCE

Left with only powdery memories of her…
…of what used to be pliable flesh against her flesh.

Instead of passion being firmly in our hands…
…we search now for vaporous happiness…
…for absolutes… that will live beyond now.

We hope for the bleeding to continue in our heart…
…as proof of eternity… even in pain.

We search for absolutes and try to believe.
So… with an agnostic heart… we enter the temple of Hope and Remembrance.

And thus we hope that we will continue to live as soul next to her soul.
Only to realize that love… like sorrow… does not know eternity.

We search for absolutes… and find instead an empty place next to us.
We want to remember… and yet scurry for fading pictures in shoeboxes.
We want things to last… and tearfully we forget the face of our own mother.

We want to touch again the passion… and fearfully realize that…
…the sight of our object of desire…
…is our own… in a lonely mirror.

And so… in the temple of absolutes…
…we give one last look at the altar of solidity.
With a blasphemous and guilty heart… parted and wanting lips… we walk out.

As we look back… the edifice of things
That gives us Hope and Remembrance collapses.
It collapses of our own actions.
Its foundations attacked by our weakness
In front of the pain of separation and loneliness.

This beautiful edifice to her love and name is now a symbol of our loss.
Our eyes cannot bear to be reminded of its precious value.
We turn away and try to shout her name in front of its steeples.

The worn out steps leading to the portals
Are crushed by the stones of temporal reality.
And so… through the tears and the dust…
…we are amazed to hear no sound coming from our throat.

For in this world of cold and everyday responsibilities...
...even the deepest sobs... the bloodiest wounds...
...the most cherished faces and memories...
...go... silently to the dustbins of time past.

We hope for merciful *death* itself to be an absolute...
        ...as we nonchalantly gaze at an elegant swan...

...when we are suddenly brought back to reality...
        ...on this weathered bench...
...by the salty taste on our tearful cheeks.

We remember then... what brought us to this place:
        ...we are alone.

And thus we learn the truth.
We learn why lovers close their eyes when they kiss...
...that it is our body's way to live in... and remember the moment.

And we learn the hard lesson that...
...the absolute does live...
        ...and unfortunately for lovers...
                ...in absolute emptiness.

We feel guilt upon realizing that the faces we have loved, even that of our beloved mother, disappear with time.

GLOSSARY

This glossary of words, names and terms is added for the convenience of readers to enhance their enjoyment of and access to the full range of language and meaning used in the poems. Many of Jean-Yves Solinga's poems are translations from French and are littered with words of particular cultural and literary reference from this language. There are also religious and historical references and other terms which may be unfamiliar to some readers. The briefest definition or explanation is provided only to support the meaning in the poem. Of course alternative definitions exist and these can be found in any good dictionary, thesaurus or encyclopedia. The glossary is presented in alphabetical order to avoid the need to repeat words that appear in more than one poem.

Absurdism: see **Camus**.

Adulterous Wife: by Albert Camus. This is a lyrically and philosophically powerful passage where a wife leaves her husband in the inn's bedroom at night to climb to the parapets overlooking the desert and experiences "nuptials" with the setting.

Au Départ de Saint Michel: A bistro-restaurant at the Saint Michel Bridge in Paris.

Avenue des roches: The location of the Solinga family house in Marseille.

Baba au rum: A rum alcohol soaked pastry.

Balzac, Honoré de: He is the author of *The Girl with the Golden Eyes,* the tale of an hypnotically beautiful woman.

Baudelaire, Charles: A 19th century poet whose setting is often the Paris of his self destruction. Beautifully described in *Flowers of Evil*. Known also for his lyrical prose.

Bled: A Moroccan term for the country side. It is also the term used in the French lexicon for arid or empty landscape.

Bonne Mère: [Good Mother] A term of endearment for the statue of the Virgin Mary at the top of Notre Dame de la Garde; the Basilica overlooking the harbor of Marseille.

Brassens, Georges, A French singer who wrote at times unfettered lyrics criticizing French authorities and taboos.

Camus, Albert: An agnostic writer and moralist of the Absurd. A philosophy where man confronts his consciousness [see: **crise** and **prise de conscience**] of the meaninglessness of life. Best known for *The Stranger* whose main character exemplifies the consciousness of the Absurd. Camus is part of a long line of moralists who try to deal with good and evil in their vision of a godless universe.

César, Fanny and Marius: This is a trilogy by Marcel Pagnol that captures early twentieth century life of Marseille. César, Marius' father is the anchor of the group. Fanny is in love with the childhood friend and adventurous Marius. Marius succumbs to the need to see the world; but unknowingly leaves Fanny with child. Powerful reconstruction of the people and neighborhood of the author's parents generation.

Château d'If: This is the island facing Marseille. It is the location for the story of *The Count of Monte Cristo*. Also reputed, among other places, to be where the *Man in the Iron Mask* was held.

Chiaroscuro: This is an Italian term for a painting technique that splits the canvas into light and dark tones in a dramatic way. Clair-obscur is the French translation.

Chimène: see **Corneille**

[The] Christ of Vigny: The figure of the Christ of the Passion as seen by Alfred de Vigny [19th century French poet] in the Garden of Gethsemane as abandoned by his Father and questioning his fate.

Corneille: A playwright of classical French tragedies. *Le Cid* - El Cid – studies the dilemma of Rodrigue who must keep his honor by killing his future father-in-law to remain worthy of Chimène and thus risk losing her in the process. Hence the "Corneillean" dilemma.

Corniche: The name of a cliff hugging road along the Mediterranean.

Crise de conscience: This is the name of the first step in the philosophical world where man "becomes aware" of the contradiction of his status as a consciousness versus a blind, inert universe.

Dali, Salvador: A surrealist painter known for his representation of 'melted' objects. Hence the visual reference in the text.

Delacroix: see **Women of Algiers** in their living quarters.

Duras, Marguerite: The author of *The Lover* [L'amant] which is loosely autobiographical. Very sensual account of a sexual affair of a young French colonial girl with an older man.

El Cid: The name given to Rodrigue.

Existentialism: A philosophy championed by Sartre according to which one defines himself by, and is responsible for, his own actions. I do, therefore I am.

Fanny: see **César**

Faust: The famous story of a man who is willing to give up his soul for youth, wisdom and love.

Falafel: A popular dish of North African, middle Eastern origin found in ethnic restaurants.

Fort Notre-Dame: The name of a street in Marseille leading up to Notre-Dame de la Garde on the hill overlooking the city. It is also the street on which the author's father's was born.

Gabin, Jean: This is a famous 1940's, 1950's French actor. An actor with a very powerful screen presence.
Galatea: A statue that comes to life in the story of Pygmalion.

Gendarme: This is the name of the French government police. The Gendarme are part of the French Army; hence can be sent for overseas duty.

Gulino's: Bakery where author's mother regularly took his children for their favorite Danish pastry.

Hugo, Victor: A prolific 19th century French writer of *Les Misérables* and *Notre Dame de Paris*, better known as *The Hunchback of Notre Dame*. A famous scene in *Les Misérables* is where the Bishop sees good in Jean Valjean, a homeless convict, and sends him off with what is stolen precious silverware on the understanding that one day he, Jean, will also "give." In *Notre Dame de Paris*, Hugo describes the haunting beauty and eyes of Esmeralda, the gypsy who tempts and threatens the weaknesses of the Frollo the symbol of unjust and perverted authority. Hugo writes also about the 'duality' of man and mankind: being able to represent simultaneously elements of the 'grotesque' and the 'sublime.' For example, the physical ugliness of Quasimodo and his beautiful soul.

Impression soleil levant, [Impression Rising Sun.] The name for an iconic painting by Monet that is reputed to have giving the name to the Impressionist art movement.

Ionesco, Eugène: A Roumanian born French playwright of the Avant Garde Theatre of the Absurd of the 1950's. Ionesco had a particular talent and ease in making 'concrete' or physical ideas and thoughts, through such techniques as empty or cluttered stages. His most memorable plays are *The Bald Soprano* and *Rhinoceros*. In the latter, intolerance typical of extremist philosophies is exemplified by everyone catching the 'disease' of 'rhinoceratis.'

Labrador: A cold sea current from Canada, which passes close to New England, USA. In a number of the poems in this book, this is used as a symbolic antithesis, in the present, of the warm setting of the author's warm North African youth.

Larrabee: A student dormitory at Connecticut College, New London, Connecticut.

Liaisons [les] dangereuses [Dangerous Liaisons]: The name of a tale by L'Abbé Prévost of unscrupulous emotional and sexual abuse in high aristocratic French society.

L'île de la cité and l'île saint Louis: These are two islands in the middle of the Seine in Paris. Notre Dame de Paris is on l'île de la Cité where is also located one of the city's Jewish memorials.

Loyal: The name of an unruly horse, with this contradictory name, of the author's father as a Spahi.

Maghreb: This is an Arabic word for the "setting sun," in the West of the North African continent. Hence: Northern Africa; Morocco. Used often under adjectival form in text.

Marius: see **César**.

Marseillais: A French word for men from Marseille, a traditional city of sailors and Italian immigrants.

Montmartre: The name of a hill overlooking Paris with white basilica at the very top.

Monet, Claude: A painter whose work *"Impression soleil levant"* is supposed to have coined the term Impressionism. This painting is found in the Marmottan museum in Paris.

162

Meursault: A character in Camus' *The Stranger*, man of the absurd, par excellence. He goes through an amoral life where going to the beach, making love or killing a man are disturbingly equivalent under the heat of the sun.

Pascal, Blaise: A 17th century philosopher and writer whose Pensées - "Thoughts" – are his pro-religious positions on man's standing in the Universe. His "Wager" and his "Thinking reed" arguments are famous. The former position is 'betting' on the existence of God, just in case. The latter, on showing the ultimate value of man's consciousness in spite of his physical weakness facing an inert Universe. Pascal's *Memorial* is a reference to a sheet of paper on which Pascal put down his philosophical and religious feelings after a momentous night of reflection. He kept it the rest of his life in the lining of his clothing. It was not found until his death. It is an intimate look into his new found faith and is written in an interesting mixture of lyrical prose.

Pastis: see **Ricard**

Père Lachaise Cemetery: This is a famous cemetery East of Paris where some very famous people are buried. Jim Morrison, of "Baby, Light my Fire" fame, among them.

Place de Clichy: This is a neighborhood near la Place Blanche in Paris. Raucous area of movies houses and night spots. Not far from the Moulin Rouge.

Plane trees: This is a very popular species of tree with characteristic bark found throughout cities, villages and along roads in France.

Prise de conscience: The second step in the philosophical world where man "takes" a position vis-à-vis the awareness of the absurd.

Proust, Marcel: The author of *Remembrance of things past* whose most memorable passage is when, as an adult, the narrator's past comes to life as he tastes a Madeleine – a pastry – dunked in a cup of morning tea.

Rictus: The gaping or opening of the mouth.

Ricard: An anisette drink from Marseille.

Rimbaud, Arthur: A young, incredibly talented, French poet of the 19th century who completely gave up writing.

Rodrigue: A character of French tragedy. Courageous swordsman who fought the Moors in Spain. In love with Chimène. see **Corneille**

Rue des rosiers: Pre-World War II center of Jewish cultural and culinary life in Paris. Site of anti-Semitic deportation.

Rue paradis: The name of a street in Marseille. Ironic turn of history that this "street of Paradise" would also be the location of headquarters of the Gestapo during the war.

Sainte-Maxime: The name of a little town on the French Riviera.

Saint Pierre Cemetery: A surprisingly beautiful place in Marseille. Majestic white granite mountains in the back and the ever present cicadas trees in the pine scented heat of summer visits.

Saint Germain-des-Prés: An eleventh century church in Paris in the neighborhood of existentialist life of the fifties and sixties.

Salé: A city just North of Rabat, the capital of Morocco. This is the site of a beautiful Kasbha. Next to Sidi Moussa.

Sartre, Jean-Paul: An atheist philosopher of Existentialism. In *Huis clos*, translated as *No Exit*, he studies the glance and judgment of the Other as hellish. Usually a cold analytic writer; but in *Les mots*, his biographical work, he shows a softer view of the role of his reader as one who gives him some continuation in Time.

Sidi Moussa: The name of Lord Moses in Arabic. Also the name of a little beach just North of Salé. According to tradition also "patron holy man" of infertile women. In this book, the author uses it as a multifaceted and idealized place of return.

Sisyphus: The name of a character of Greek mythology condemned by the gods to endlessly push a rock up a hill for having confronted their authority.

Solitary: The word in Italian is "Solinga." The author's family name was given to his orphaned grandfather who was taken in by newly arrived Italian immigrants to Southern France.

Spahi: This is the name for an elegantly uniformed horseman of a French regiment. Arguably one of the most beautiful toy soldiers seen on one of the author's many trips to Paris that sparked a poem.

Tristan and Isolt: These are the names of doomed lovers from a Medieval tale. Having taking a magic potion by accident they cannot but love each other at the risk of hurting their beloved King. Hence, they are symbols in literature of impossible and forbidden love.

Trénet, Charles: A prolific songwriter who captured in gentle melodies such subjects as Paris, the sea [la mer], traditional France [Douce France] etc.

Vieux port: Famed harbor in the center of old Marseille. Known for its noisy and colorful fish markets.

Voltaire: A French writer and philosopher. He is better known for *Candide* a tale of healthy skepticism about man's ability to better himself. He also wrote lesser known poetry. In this book the author uses this concept of the "the Voltairean glance" as inspiration for a poem upon witnessing the massive Lisbon earthquake and the helplessness of people.

Volubilis: This is the name of a 2,000 year old Roman ruin in Morocco.

Women of Algiers in their living quarters: This is the name of a painting by the Romantic artist Eugène Delacroix. It shows an exotic look at this Oriental setting with excellent use of complementary colors and attention to detail he had garnered in his quick sketches.

INDEX OF TITLES AND FIRST LINES

Titles are in italics, followed in parentheses by the poem numbers. First lines are in regular text.

www.ingramcontent.com/pod-product-compliance
Lightning Source LLC
Chambersburg PA
CBHW080530090426
42733CB00015B/2536